WHOSE JUDGMENT COUNTS?

REGIONAL RESOURCE CENTER ON DEAFNESS
EDUCATION BUILDING
WESTERN OREGON UNIVERSITY
MONMOUTH, OREGON 97361

WHOSE JUDGMENT COUNTS?

ASSESSING BILINGUAL CHILDREN, K–3

EVANGELINE HARRIS STEFANAKIS

HEINEMANN • PORTSMOUTH, NH

Heinemann
A division of Reed Elsevier Inc.
361 Hanover Street
Portsmouth, NH 03801–3912

Offices and agents throughout the world

© 1998 by Evangeline Harris Stefanakis

Library of Congress Cataloging-in-Publication Data
Stefanakis, Evangeline Harris.
    Whose judgment counts? : assessing bilingual children, K–3 /
Evangeline Harris Stefanakis.
        p. cm.
    Includes bibliographical references.
    ISBN 0-325-00011-5 (alk. paper)
    1. Linguistic minorities—Education (Primary)—Ability testing—
United States. 2. Education, Bilingual—Ability testing—United
States. 3. Educational tests and measurements—Validity—United
States. 4. Teacher-student relationships—United States.
    I. Title.
LC3725.S84   1998
370.117'5—dc21   98-12312
                                                                       CIP

Editor: William Varner
Cover design: Jenny Jensen Greenleaf
Manufacturing: Courtney Ordway

Printed in the United States of America on acid-free paper
02 01 00 99 98   DA   1 2 3 4 5

To my amazing family:
William, Irene, Manuel, Rianna, Nikias, and Alexandros
Με Αγαπη (in Greek), with Love (in English)

Contents

On teacher's judgments:

Some form of judgment on students' performance is an essential part of any learning. Informal feedback to the students—"Yes that's right," or "You might want to change this or that"—defines an important component of teaching.

In fact, students experience most evaluation as classroom feedback on their performances. Stiggins points out that 90 percent of all evaluation takes place in the classroom. This evaluation takes many forms: teachers' observations, teachers' responses to written and oral work, and informal discussion with students about their work.

RUTH MITCHELL

Acknowledgments

Many thanks to Dr. Vito Perrone, my advisor, teacher, and mentor, who listened to me and supported every step of this research. I am very grateful for his suggestions, whether I was in Cambridge, Greece, or the Czech Republic. His deep thinking and commitment to understanding teachers and teaching will remain with me as I continue to share in this important effort.

My committee members contributed their ideas, insights, and perspectives and helped me listen to what teachers were saying and what it all meant. Dr. Lilia Bartolomé shared her knowledge and practice in studying bilingual learners. Teaching, learning, and thinking with her shaped my understanding of using sociocultural research and practice to better serve diverse populations. Dr. Joseph Maxwell helped shape my research design and gave me a fundamental understanding of the endless possibilities in qualitative research. Dennie Wolf, my first teacher in the alternative assessment research field, brought me new ideas and points of view that still guide me in my daily work with teachers. My thanks to you all.

I am grateful to the many administrators and teachers in the Cambridge Public Schools who shared their talents, expertise, and energies with me. These teachers provide young children with the daily gift of "learning how to learn." To Lynn Stuart and Brenda Engel, who remain collaborators that share vital notions regarding documentation and assessment, thank you for constantly talking, reading, and writing beside me.

Thanks go to my colleagues at the Harvard Graduate School of Education: Eric Johnson, Sally Middlebrooks, Bob Menchel, Linda Nathan, Helen Snively, and Carol Pelleteir, who read transcripts, drafts, and diagrams and who constantly challenged me to keep thinking and writing. Dody Riggs, my editor and writing support person, deserves endless thanks for reading, commenting, and encouraging me through the many drafts of this thesis. Her good humor and consistent feedback motivated me at every step.

Finally, I owe my family never-ending thanks. These special people have continually supported my growing and learning: my father William, in spirit, nurtured and inspired my writing; my mother Irene taught me to appreciate two languages and cultures; my children, Rianna, Nikias, and Alexandros, patiently waited for me to be finished. My husband, Manny, remains the single most important individual to "sit beside me" and offer me whatever it took to get this work done. It is to William, Irene, Manny, and the kids that I dedicate this research. Now it's my turn, more freely, to sit beside them.

Introduction

My interest in classroom assessment stems from my experience as a bilingual speaker, teacher, and special educator. For nineteen years, in public and private elementary classrooms in the United States and overseas, I struggled with the standardized instruments used to assess young children. These tests, normed on native English speakers, were the only tools available to assess and place bilingual children in regular or special education classes. I faced the inherent contradiction of using linguistically and culturally biased tests to evaluate the abilities of bilingual children. Like many teachers, I needed expertise in assessing bilingual children in terms of their individual talents.

I recall a girl named Arnet, a sixth grader who arrived in my classroom, drooling, dazed, and nonverbal. Despite many efforts to engage her in the classroom activities, she remained unresponsive for almost seven months. Arnet spoke no English, but her parents insisted that she had been an excellent student in her native language. The school psychologist, speech therapist, counselor, and administrators had evaluated her with tests, and she was declared "below average in intelligence with severe educational and psychological problems." Our team had none of her previous school records, only parental reports to draw on.

One day, as I started to read the fairy tale *Cinderella* to a group of children, she motioned to me that she wanted the book. I handed it to her. She stood up in front of our group and articulately read this story that she knew and adored to the class—*in English*. I was aghast that we could have pronounced her "limited in potential" as a result of *our* "limited" methods of educational assessment of bilingual children.

Little research was available to help practitioners like myself develop informal, nondiscriminatory assessments for children like Arnet. Through trial and error, I developed my own informal assessment methods, including observations and multiple interviews, to record more effectively how bilingual children responded to classroom activities. When making difficult decisions about placements or instructional programs, I learned to combine formal assessments with a variety of informal assessments to deal with the complexity of understanding a child's language proficiency and cognitive skills.

My own years of practice in schools have taught me that teacher expertise is often undervalued in the decision-making process for all children, and especially for bilingual children. In diagnosing learning problems, specialists who give tests are seen as the experts, while teachers are seen merely as the technicians who carry out instructional plans designed by others. As a special needs teacher, I found that teachers' assessments provided a vital perspective on children and their learning potential.

To learn more about the assessment of bilingual children, I returned to the classroom to look more closely at teachers whose expertise had not been documented for practitioners or researchers. The teachers I studied had a wealth of experience as practitioners who

> understand that bilingualism can be an asset, not a liability, which
> means they look at the learner and his native language initially
> from a position of strength. Two essential assessment questions are:
> "What does the child already know?" and "How does he or she
> learn?" (Cummins 1989, 286)

My aim was to learn by *sitting beside* classroom experts who struggle to better understand the language and the culture of diverse learners. I wanted to understand *classroom assessment as the teacher sitting beside the learner* in his or her learning environment.

The research in this book is intended for a wide audience within the educational community—those interested in how better to assess and teach the diverse learners in today's classrooms. The title, *Whose Judgment Counts?* comes from the words of a Boston teacher who told me:

> Whose judgment counts when it comes to assessing bilingual children in Boston schools? It is usually the school psychologist. . . . Their expertise in assessment—that is, *in giving tests*—is seen as the judgment that counts.
>
> If you really want to learn about assessing bilingual children, ask the classroom teachers who have years of strategies behind them to use. After about three weeks in my classroom, I can usually tell what a child needs and how best to teach them even if they speak little English. (Narrative summary 1994)

This book describes successful classroom assessment strategies used by a group of highly skilled urban teachers who share what they know about assessing young bilingual children. These teachers' success stories capture the intricacies of daily classroom assessment and provide real-life examples for other teachers who seek to understand the learning *abilities*, rather than the *disabilities*, of bilingual children.

Related political, social, and cultural issues in teachers' classroom assessment are also brought to the forefront through the stories of these teachers' struggles and successes.

Whose Judgment Counts? guides the reader through these informal assessments of young children, using the teachers' own voices to describe how they evaluate minority language students. This is especially important because

> teachers [in schools today] need ways of establishing their authority as evaluators of their *own* students in their *own* classrooms and having that judgment count for more than a classroom grade. (Mitchell 1992, 137)

As a teacher first and a researcher second, I have never stopped thinking about Arnet, who was such a puzzle to me and my colleagues. Without knowing it, I had misjudged this child and her family. As educators dealing with bilingual learners struggle to learn how to best assess and teach them, they may find that the closer they look, the more the child will surprise them and the more they will learn.

Teachers need to continue to look, listen, ask questions, and compile student work to better know who their bilingual students are, and then what they know and can do. It is to our educational community, both teachers and researchers, who continue to wrestle with issues of language and learning, that I address this story.

1

Whose Judgment Counts When Assessing Bilingual Children?

Why Study Teachers?

UNDERSTANDING THE COMPLEXITY
OF ASSESSING BILINGUAL CHILDREN

The verb *to assess* finds its roots in the Latin *assidere,* meaning "to sit beside." I define *assessment* as an interactive process that provides authentic and meaningful feedback for improving student learning, teachers' instructional practice, and educational options in the classroom. Understanding the nature of educational assessment involves looking carefully at the interaction between teacher and learner as they sit beside one another. As Stephanie Pace Marshall (1992) states:

> Assessment is not an end in itself. It is a process that facilitates appropriate instructional decisions by providing information on two fundamental questions: How are *we* (teacher and learner) doing? and how can *we* (teacher and learner) do better? (3)

Assessing the language and learning abilities of a child from a different linguistic and cultural background is a complex task. It raises important questions about a practitioner's knowledge, skills, and attitudes. Sorting out these questions is a first step in examining how primary teachers assess bilingual students.

How *do* most primary classroom teachers of bilingual children carry out this process? How *do* these teachers take into account what happens to a child at home or on the playground on any given day? What impact does the setting (home, classroom, office) have on a young child's behavior during assessment? What tools and strategies do these teachers use to carry out the assessment? Does the teacher utilize an advocacy approach to assessment, searching for the strengths of that child (Cummins 1986), or is the assessment process one of unequal power relations between an adult and a child?

In 1922, Paul Davis Chapman portrayed the assessment process using the image of a powerful assessor (an adult representing education) looking at the population of young and diverse learners through a magnifying glass of intelligence tests to determine their educational pathway (see Figure 1-1).

What the assessor (or educator) sees while looking carefully at an individual child is affected by many components of the assessment process. In the foreground, we see the new method, in which an educational assessor uses intelligence tests to examine the individual child. This examination is based on a set of educational theories depicted by the books in the illustration—a scientific method of investigation, a psychology of individuality, and mental forces. The image of individualized assessment is juxtaposed with the old method, depicted on the left side of the illustration. The old method is one in which education applies guesswork or rules to sort groups of children into classes of As, Bs, or Cs.

The illustration reminds us that today we are still facing the same questions as in Chapman's time: Are we, as educators, focused on individuals or on groups when we look at bilingual children today? How do we sort students according to their language and learning abilities? Historically, assessment was considered a process of individually sorting children into groups using either a scientific or formal approach, or a less scientific or "informal" approach. Today we know that the process of assessing bilingual children is much more complicated. As Chapman shows, *the background of the person* who is "looking through the glass" affects how that person sees the student. *The relationship of the assessor to the learner* also affects what that person sees: Is the assessor a psycholo-

Figure 1–1 *School as Sorters*

gist or an educational specialist (trained to study individual behavior) who has never met the child previously? Is the assessor a classroom teacher who is familiar with studying individuals as part of a group and who is with the child daily?

In addition, *each potential assessor brings a different lens,* a different kind of expertise with which to look at the learning abilities of a bilingual child. The assessors' expertise determines (a) how they approach the assessment process; (b) whether they select formal or informal assessment tools; (c) how long they spend with the child; and even (d) where they assess the child (classroom, office, playground).

Finally, my own practice has taught me that *the context* of the learning environment is a key element in understanding what any young child knows, especially a bilingual child. The closer and more frequently assessors look, the more they refine their "magnifying glass" image of the language and learning abilities of a bilingual child. A classroom teacher who sees a child each day collects many "episodes of learning" (Wolf 1989), providing a much fuller picture of the child's strengths and weaknesses. Through this lens the teacher can develop his or her own assessment of that child's knowledge of language and literacy.

WHY LEARN ABOUT TEACHERS' CLASSROOM ASSESSMENT?

An understanding of teachers' effective classroom assessment is vital to researchers and practitioners. Despite the increasing numbers of students from diverse backgrounds, there are no books describing *how* classroom teachers make sense of the learning and language differences of young children. Research indicates that teachers often misidentify bilingual children as language or learning disabled, when in reality they are simply limited in English proficiency:

> Minority over-representation in special education continues. . . .
> Once a referral [by classroom teachers] is made, the likelihood of testing is high, and once testing takes place, strong gravitational forces toward special education placement are in motion.
>   The referral to assessment to placement rates oscillate between 75 and 90 percent. (Ambert 1991, 269)

> This means that once a bilingual child is referred for testing, that same child is placed in special education about 85 percent of the time. Furthermore, once a child is placed in special education, despite a mistaken assessment, it takes them on average six years to get out. (Ambert 1991, 269)

My experience with Arnet, who spoke no English but read *Cinderella* perfectly, happened to be in an international school where special education laws did not apply. We quickly saw our misjudgment and placed her in regular education classes. American public schools are clearly not so quick to correct educational placement errors for bilingual children whose parents may not understand the system's decision making.

Many bilingual researchers believe that the misplacement of bilingual children into special education continues because teachers who are confused about how to assess these children refer them for testing to be freed of the responsibility (Baca and Almanza 1991; Damico 1991). This dangerous practice of *testing to find a disability must stop*, and can only be addressed by better informing teachers about alternative assessment practices. The research and practitioner communities are confused about assessment and this is affecting bilingual children.

> Information for researchers, educators, and parents is needed on the best assessment practices for bilingual children . . . practices that give teachers and students actual feedback on teaching and learning. All school practitioners will need training in techniques . . . such as observation, interviewing, and in linking assessment with instruction. (Ambert 1991, 358)

By understanding more about alternative assessment, teachers, as the primary agents of assessment and referral, can play a key role as agents of change and can stop inappropriate referrals of bilingual students to special education. As Baca and Almanza (1991) suggest:

> Teachers are the most valuable resource. When they are empowered with current instructional and research information and the latest . . . strategies, they can facilitate the optimal cognitive and affective development of culturally and linguistically different students. (26)

WHY CREATE TEACHER PORTRAITS?

The stories and portraits in this book describe how "effective primary teachers" informally assess the language and literacy skills of bilingual students during daily instruction. The term "effective teachers" refers to a select group of veteran practitioners recommended by various colleagues—administrators, principals, fellow teachers—as being skilled in the informal assessment of bilingual students. These teachers were enthusiastic collaborators, eager to share information about the processes they use. Hopefully their ideas will inspire colleagues who also wrestle with issues of language and learning in young bilingual children.

In these descriptions, I use a sociocultural framework to help describe the complexity of assessing both second-language proficiency and cognitive learning. Taking a sociocultural approach means looking critically at the interaction between teacher and learner in order to understand the political, social, cultural, and intellectual factors involved. Three questions guided my inquiry:

1. How do teachers in this study informally assess the language and literacy skills of bilingual children in their classrooms?
2. How do teachers link assessment of language and literacy skills to instruction for these children?
3. What reasons do teachers give for assessing bilingual students as they do?

To address these questions, I collected and analyzed observational and interview data about these teachers, and over time developed case studies describing their classroom assessment practices. These case studies, or portraits, present both the process of monolingual and bilingual teachers' classroom assessment and the context in which the process occurs: the daily life of the classroom.

2

What Research Suggests About Assessing Young Bilingual Children

The educational literature from 1987 to 1996 suggests that assessment practice is evolving from a standardized product format to a more complex, problem-solving process (Stefanakis 1993). My research supports this change, indicating that assessment practice for young bilingual children should be multifaceted and involve multiple perspectives. Further, it suggests that assessment techniques should seek to understand the interactions between teacher and learner in the context of natural settings, such as classrooms, rather than in unfamiliar clinical settings.

THE CHANGING FIELD OF EDUCATIONAL ASSESSMENT IN SCHOOLS

There is a growing movement in the United States and abroad to reform assessment in schools in response to changes in educational theory and classroom practice. Reports from both the National Assessment of Educational Progress (NAEP) and the International Comparative Assessment (ICA) indicate growing dissatisfaction with what American and international students know and can do.

7

Educators are looking for more direct and continuous evidence of student learning than is provided by standardized testing. Moreover, they are recognizing that standardized testing fails to describe the intricacy of individual student learning in today's classrooms.

Reform movements in Australia, Canada, Great Britain, and the Netherlands parallel American assessment reform efforts (Baron 1991; OECD 1992). Looking at state and local efforts in the United States and abroad provides further evidence of an international quest for new forms of assessment that will simultaneously better serve students, teachers, and policy makers (Baron 1992; French 1991). Initiatives to create alternative formats for local and state assessment have been undertaken in Arizona, California, Connecticut, Kentucky, Maryland, and Vermont.

The overall goals of assessment reform in the United States and abroad are (1) for students to be able to monitor their own progress; (2) for teachers to be able to make informed decisions about their students' level of understanding; and (3) for policy makers to have access to accurate accountability data that measures the skills and applications of learning valued by society (Baron 1992; Wolf 1989). Practitioners and researchers acknowledge the need to have multiple formats and individual perspectives represented in the assessment process.

To accomplish these goals, educational assessment reforms focus on the authenticity of assessment, the standards against which to measure student performance, and the training of educators to use alternative formats (French 1992). Assessment should be:

1. aligned with *what is taught and how it is taught;*
2. *ongoing and over time;*
3. *embedded in the instructional process.*

Time will determine the outcomes of these new assessment practices for schools.

THE EVOLVING ROLE OF TEACHERS

As the field of assessment changes, so does the role of teachers who are responsible for determining its pathways. Many teachers do not understand the shortcomings of psychometric or formal assessment instruments and procedures, and thus they tend to confuse language proficiency issues with real special education needs (Ambert 1991;

Genesee 1994; Damico 1991). Teachers may misinterpret test results because many standardized instruments and techniques are culturally and linguistically biased due to their language and format (Baca and Almanza 1991; Figueroa 1989). Unfortunately, teachers possess few reliable tools for assessing bilingual students and for making informed judgments on referrals, placements, and instruction.

Cummins (1991) describes the lingering barriers of psychometrics and standardized testing, which tend to label bilingual children as disabled:

> Recent studies suggest that despite an appearance of change (PL 94-142), psychologists continue to test bilingual children until they find a "disability" to explain the student's apparent academic difficulty. (14)

To reverse the "legitimizing function of assessment" and to stop mislabeling bilingual children as special needs, Cummins urges educators to:

1. incorporate a child's language and culture into assessment and instruction;
2. encourage children to use both first and second languages to actively amplify interaction with peers and adults;
3. collaborate with parents in shared assessment practices.

Until educators recognize and include political, social, cultural, and linguistic factors as part of the assessment process, it remains a potentially discriminatory practice when applied to bilingual children.

ASSESSMENT AS A SOCIOCULTURAL PROCESS

The traditional psychometric model for assessing all children consists of a collection of standardized instruments and techniques to diagnose language and learning problems. These psychometric instruments assume that the learning deficit is *in the child.* This is in contrast to a sociocultural approach, which assumes that each child presents an example of difference and complexity, and that understanding a child's *difference,* not *deficits,* is the role of educational assessment.

A sociocultural perspective assumes that children learn language in real-life situations that depend on social interactions and that bilingual children display different knowledge and use of language, depending on the social context. In support of this view, Snow (1992) argues that "the critical insights of the sociocultural perspective must be introduced if we are to have adequate assessment of bilingual individuals or evaluation of bilingual programs" (16).

The sociocultural perspective makes three assumptions:

1. Bilingualism is a potential cognitive asset that can enhance learning. (Hakuta and Garcia 1989)
2. Sociocultural factors (political, social, cultural, and linguistic) can affect language learning, and context is the key to understanding language output. (Snow 1992)
3. Language proficiency and related learning abilities should be assessed in context and over time. (Baca and Almanza 1991; Damico 1991; Snow 1992)

As Snow further explains:

> Whereas other approaches identify a linguistic norm . . . toward which the learner is clearly moving, sociocultural approaches recognize the social nature of language use and the impossibility of identifying better or worse varieties of any language.
>
> Sociocultural approaches are particularly helpful in understanding the social and cultural pressures affecting learners in situations where different social value is attached to their two languages. (16)

This review therefore looks at assessment through a sociocultural lens. Acknowledging that language is a sociocultural phenomenon as well as a cognitive achievement allows for understanding the language and the culture of the student and tailoring an assessment process to fit that student. The focus is on recognizing *the different learning abilities* of bilingual students in a given context, using that information to look more closely at the interaction among student, teacher, and learning environment, and finally assessing the child's literacy skills.

FORMAL ASSESSMENT: THE MOVE TO A COMPREHENSIVE APPROACH

Educational assessment of bilingual children, including assessment of their language proficiency and cognitive learning, is a controversial topic in research literature. Formal assessment—standardized, normed evaluation—presupposes that the child must meet an expected norm of educational performance, and if he or she does not, then remediation is needed. The process is taken as a "given," as a socially and politically neutral process, when in reality it is not. Studies from 1987 to 1996 agree that the process of formal assessment for linguistic minority students needs careful scrutiny in terms of

1. bias in test data interpretation;
2. construct validity of tests in translation (how they were put together);
3. the cultural bias of test items and vocabulary used;
4. the child's previous experience in test taking.

Although single research studies indicate that standardized tests may be valid and reliable (Bracken Concept Test, Woodcock Johnson Psycho Educational Battery), the consensus of recent research on formal assessment of bilingual students indicates that it is critical to understand the limitations of the standardized test instruments and the complexity of understanding the language competency of the bilingual child.

When applying formal assessments, the following educational implications should be considered:

- Bilingual students *take more time* to complete tasks in their second language, so performance on timed tests may be invalid.
- Bilingual students may *use a different reasoning strategy* according to their native language so that a systematic, sequential testing approach may be unfamiliar and of questionable validity.
- Careful evaluation of native language proficiency (using both formal and informal assessments) *must precede* any assessment of learning potential.
- Decision making related to bilingual students should be made from a collection of formal and informal assessments in both the native language (L1) *and* English (L2).

A comprehensive process for the assessment of bilingual children concurs with the call by researchers such as Dolson (1994) and Snow (1992) for a sociocultural approach to bilingual education. Baca (Baca and Clark 1992) explains the shift in the bilingual assessment field from creating tests in translation to redefining the testing process:

I thought that if we could fix the assessment issues of reliability and validity, then we would be providing nondiscriminatory assessment.

Baca's words below echo the reactions of bilingual researchers who, from 1986 to 1992, focused on renorming tests for Asians, Native Americans, Blacks, Hispanics, and other minority groups in the United States:

25 percent of the bias is in the instruments
75 percent of the bias is in the humans and the process factors of assessment.

THE LITERATURE ON INFORMAL ASSESSMENT

An alternative viewpoint and definition surround issues of informal assessment. Informal assessment assumes that assessment is the process of gathering, interpreting, and synthesizing information to aid in decision making about children (Airasian 1991). Informal assessments are designed to gather specific information in two ways: by watching a child (observing); and by talking to a child (interviewing).

Observation

Observation is highly regarded in research literature on the assessment of bilingual children (Ambert 1991; Rhodes 1993). It has proved a useful tool for educational, behavioral, and language assessment of young children, particularly those with developing language abilities, because it is flexible, can tap nonlanguage behavior, and can view the child in any learning context over time.

Figueroa (1990b) believes that observation is the most useful and informative of current language assessment approaches to use with linguistic minority children. For understanding a child's language abilities, he finds observation more useful than home language surveys or standardized tests because of its flexibility and adaptability. Most bilingual researchers propose three observational formats for assessing the language skills of young bilingual children:

1. dialogues with the child in L1 and L2;
2. interviews with teachers, parents, and peers describing their observations of the child's formal and informal communication skills;
3. observations of the child's language use in activities that involve play.

Current research on informal assessment of cognition also focuses on combining observational formats to assess more accurately what children know. Suggestions for cognitive assessment focus on using a selection of checklists or guided forms to record what children do. Anthony et al. (1991) point out that checklists remind a teacher what to observe, and more easily inform others of the kinds of behaviors that are valued in a classroom. Checklists for assessing language, literacy, numeracy, problem solving, and learning style are available in the research of Airasian (1991), Anthony et al. (1991), and Tierney, Carter, and Desai (1991). Anthony et al. (1991) remind educators that commercial checklists are rarely as valuable as those developed by teachers themselves for a given context. The danger inherent in any checklist is that it is restrictive and may produce tunnel vision in those who use it.

Interviews

Interviews collected from children, parents, teachers, and other school personnel can be a viable way to gather information about a child's strengths and weaknesses from a variety of perspectives. Interviews that view the whole child can describe a child's background, including developmental history, previous education, health, family, household data, language use patterns, coping, and support systems, as well as current classroom performance.

Damico et al. (1992) advocate the use of a framework to carry out language assessment focused on social situations, and on situations of academic interaction between child, teacher, or activity. They provide a series of interview checklists that serve as checks and balances to help gather information about conversational ability and academic language comprehension. For more descriptive language assessment, they suggest combinations of:

- a survey of factors that affect test performance (family, community, school, classroom, and students);
- a native language survey that interviews significant people in the child's life: at home, at school, and with peers;
- a teacher interview that considers L1 and L2 oral language and literacy;
- an interview recording the teacher's instruction language;
- an interview of home bilingual usage for parents.

WHAT THE LITERATURE SAYS ABOUT
FORMAL AND INFORMAL ASSESSMENT

Recent literature on bilingual and early childhood education suggests that because bilingualism is a complex and multifaceted cognitive asset (Alvarez 1991; Ambert 1991; Hakuta and Garcia 1989; Hernandez 1994; Snow 1992), there are no simple answers for how best to assess bilingual students. International studies point out the advantages of bilingualism for young children, including positive motivation and attitude for language use (Chang 1988; Vilke 1988) as well as stronger linguistic and cognitive skills in word knowledge and vocabulary (Chang 1988; Dodson and Thomas 1988). But research also warns that the educational research community has yet to identify formal assessment tools that can capture the complexities of young children's language and culture.

Current studies recommend that an assessment of native language proficiency precedes creating any format for evaluating bilingual children (Dolson 1994; Hernandez 1994; LaCelle-Peterson and Rivera 1994; Wilkinson and Holzman 1988). This can be done through formal and informal language sampling (Alvarez 1991; Fradd, Barona, and De Barona 1989; Ortiz and Garcia 1989). When assessing young bilingual children, these studies suggest, consider the context (where) and the content (what) of what children say and do. Formal and informal assessment practice should look carefully at the interaction between the child and teachers, peers, and parents.

As stated earlier, formal assessment tools and procedures for language proficiency and cognitive abilities, as a single measure, lack validity and reliability for bilingual students (Alvarez 1991; Ambert 1991; Baca and Almanza 1991; Damico et al. 1991; LaCelle-Peterson and Rivera 1994). Some tests in translation have technical aspects of validity, but are not open-ended enough to capture the complexity of a bilingual child's language and learning strengths (Baca 1992; Bracken and Fouyad 1989; Padilla, Valadez, and Chang 1988).

Many researchers, among them Dolson (1994), Figueroa (1989), Skinner (1994), Wilkinson and Holzman (1988), warn against using a single, standardized instrument for decision making with young bilingual students. Assessment of bilingual students should focus on the *process* (how a child learns, under what conditions, and with what materials), not on the single-session assessment *products* (individual test results and grade equivalent scores).

Cummins (1984), Genesee (1994), and Langdon (1989) document the difficulty that teachers and specialists have in distinguishing between a language issue and a learning disability in bilingual children. Alvarez (1991) and Duran (1991) claim that the use of standardized language assessment has proved inadequate in assessing students' dual language abilities. Baca and Almanza (1991) call for context-based assessment based on language acquisition theory:

> If one hypothesizes . . . that language learning is facilitated by comprehensible input, in context-embedded situations (like classrooms) . . . then it is logical for the language assessment tools to be structured in the same way. (15)

Overall, bilingual and early childhood researchers recommend *using a wider lens* in looking at assessment practice with bilingual children. This means combining formal and informal assessment procedures to assess language proficiency and cognitive abilities (Alvarez 1991; Ambert 1991; Baca and Clark 1992; Genishi and Brainard 1995; Ortiz and Garcia 1989). It means adding information from standardized test results through observations, interviews, and school records. And it means combining formal and informal measures to balance the needs of system-level compliance (formal) with "child-centered" (informal and classroom) assessment (Baca and Clark 1992; DeLeon 1992; Dolson 1994; Genishi and Brainard 1995; Stefanakis 1991; Ortiz 1991).

THE LITERATURE ON CLASSROOM ASSESSMENT

Researchers agree that to understand and adequately assess a bilingual child's language and learning, it is critical to see both the process and products of the child's work. This implies that classroom assessment is of vital importance and that teachers' classroom assessments are often careful judgments that should be considered in the educational assessment of bilingual children. Classroom assessment is based on the assumption that classrooms are social systems where formal instruction is one of the activities taking place. Airasian (1991) divides classroom assessment into three categories: (1) official assessment; (2) instructional assessment; and (3) sizing up, or social assessment. In *official* or formal assessment, the teacher is making system-level decisions related to promotion, grading, special placements, and achievement. In *instructional* assessment, the teacher is making decisions about what content will be taught, how content will be taught, what materials will be used, and how students are responding to what is taught. In *sizing up,* or *social* assessment, the teacher is getting an idea about students' learning styles and interactions in groups in order to facilitate daily decision making about instruction.

Alvarez (1991) refers to these classroom assessment approaches as "assessment embedded in instruction" (284), which is defined as a set of sequential testing and teaching strategies that are part of the daily curriculum for all children. These strategies are directly linked to daily classroom instruction and focus on the setting, the pedagogy, and the process of teacher-student interaction.

Ecological Assessment

Ecological assessment means the teacher designs methods for gathering observational and interview information and adds consideration of the context in which the assessment takes place. In other words, practitioners attempt to understand the individual in the context of the learning environment by analyzing both the setting and what the child does and says. Multifaceted interactions between child, teacher, peers, and the learning environment are documented in order to understand individual performance.

Curriculum-based Assessment (CBA)

CBA looks at the process of classroom interactions and can be conducted through a series of performance tasks designed by teachers that are linked to regular classroom activities. Wilkinson (1992) defines curriculum-based assessment as a procedure for determining the student's instructional needs, based on ongoing performance in an existing classroom context.

Portfolio Assessment

Portfolio assessment looks at the products of classroom interactions and is a collection of assessment material throughout the school year, which may include children's work samples, teachers' observations, student self-assessments, and reports of student-teacher conferences. Often the teacher and student together select work samples to include in the developing student's portfolio, so both engage in assessing change and growth over time. There are a limited number of references citing the use of portfolios with young bilingual students; however, the systemwide use of classroom portfolios is being developed and researched in several states, for example, Kentucky, Connecticut, and Vermont (Baron 1992).

Periodic reviews by teachers, students, and parents help recognize growth and direct the emphasis of future teaching. Comments from periodic reviews by parents and teachers are often added to the student's portfolio of collected work samples. Johnson et al. (1991) and Tierney, Carter, and Desai (1991) describe portfolio assessment designs used with early childhood and bilingual populations in the United States and Canada. They elaborate on ways to use portfolios for classroom and systemwide assessment.

Portfolios compiled in schools vary widely (Defina 1994; Valencia 1991). Generally, students select writing samples, poems, stories, artwork, classroom projects, assignments, and tests to keep as their own personal documentation. In some cases, students also keep track of books and other text materials they have read, and share written reactions with their teachers or classmates (Tierney, Carter, and Desai 1991). At the same time, a teacher may use literacy development checklists or other record keeping methods to report on observations of student progress. Students' self-evaluations of work in progress are often included in portfolios (Graves et al. 1991). Matthews (1990) reports on teachers who keep audiotapes of students reading in their portfolios.

Valencia (1990, 1994) outlines the strengths of using portfolios for bilingual children as follows:

1. It deals with authentic texts representing actual classroom reading.
2. It captures the process of learning over time.
3. It is multidimensional and represents student thinking, drafting, revision, and reflection.
4. It is based on active collaboration between teacher and students, and sometimes parents.

Portfolio assessment is particularly effective for bilingual populations because it is personalized and based on the multiple intelligences of individuals.

CONCLUSION

Overall, the research on formal, informal, and classroom assessment in early childhood bilingual education from 1987 to 1996 points to a change in the philosophy of assessment for young bilingual children. In the United States, this move is away from formal assessment toward informal assessment (Baron 1991; French 1991; Genesee and Hamayan 1994; Hernandez 1994; Wolf 1989). The trend is to create assessment tools that more accurately reflect learning in context (Baca and Clark 1992; Baron 1991; Damico et al. 1992; French 1991) and to limit bias in the process of assessing bilingual children, by using a combination of criterion-referenced tests, teacher-made tests, performance tasks, cloze tests in content areas, and learning-style tasks.

Similarly, researchers call for a process approach to assessing young bilingual children that requires information from specialists, teachers, and family members (Baca and Clark 1992; Damico et al. 1992; DeLeon 1990; Dolson 1994; Wilkinson 1992). Whether labeled "authentic assessment" or "alternative assessment," the goal is to gather information from a variety of sources while working in collaboration with the learner.

3

Teachers Preparing Themselves to Assess Bilingual Children

CLASSROOM ASSESSMENT INCLUDES THINKING AND PLANNING PRIOR TO ASSESSING

The position of the teacher—sitting beside the learner—is key to understanding how effective teachers informally assess the diverse learners in their classrooms. The questions that Stephanie Pace Marshall (1992) asks are critical:

How are *we* (teacher and learner) doing? and
how can *we* do better? (3)

The following chapters describe the experiences of six teachers: Carol, Kathy, Manuel, Betty, Hannah, and Marina. These six teachers judge not only *how their students* are doing and could do better, but also *how they, as teachers,* could more effectively assess and teach these students. To deal with the complex social, linguistic, and cultural factors involved in evaluating bilingual children, they use a process that includes thinking and planning for assessment, then performing the assessment with the bilingual student, as depicted in Figure 3-1.

19

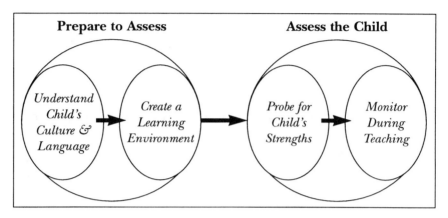

Figure 3–1 *Sociocultural Assessment Process*

For these teachers, informal assessment of bilingual students is a process of understanding how a child is learning in the cultural and social context of what naturally occurs in the classroom. Although they indicate that no single formula applies to how they individually assess the language and literacy skills of bilingual students, a sociocultural framework and a common core of practices guide their assessment and instruction and is apparent as they describe their reflective preparation and the subsequent themes and strategies they employ in the classroom.

Theme 1: Understanding Issues of Language and Culture

The six teachers agree that understanding issues of language and culture is a critical component of assessing and teaching bilingual children. It is the first step toward improving their own assessment practices and is an ongoing process that involves people in the community, school staff, curricular centers, and library facilities. The four basic strategies of this process are listed below:

1. Accept and value the bilingual learner.
2. Study the student's cultural and linguistic background.
3. Recognize the differences in home and school cultures.
4. Recognize the cultural transitions and other support.

Accept and value the bilingual learner. Kathy, Betty, Hannah, and their colleagues consider themselves detectives who try to uncover the strengths of non-English speakers. All six teachers say that they start with the premise that all children can learn if provided with an environment that supports the learning process. Manuel summarizes this idea:

> I want that child first to feel confident and happy in the environment, and if that means little language output . . . that's OK. . . . I am looking to create a community of learners. . . . I believe that no child can fail . . . so, I just go for it.

Betty, Manuel, and Hannah have positive attitudes toward bilingualism and high expectations for bilingual children. Hannah explains:

> I am very careful about the choices of words I use because the child that is bilingual has more language, not less.
> They are fluent in their native language and they are acquiring a second language. There are more demands, more cognitive things happening, so our expectations have to be adjusted, not in expecting less, but expecting more, but doing it in ways that are understanding of kids, because there are no limitations. There is potential in all children.

Study the student's cultural and linguistic background. These teachers say that they often turn to parents to help them translate puzzling behavior of children from various cultural groups. Five of the six teachers indicate that they make an effort to learn about a child's family and cultural background in order to better interpret the child's actions and teach the child most effectively. Betty, Kathy, and Hannah maintain a dialogue with parents in an attempt to work with them to help the bilingual child.

As Kathy describes, "I find out first of all if there is a resource somewhere in the school system that could help me have a discussion with the parents. I try to keep a daily dialogue with parents." Betty notes how difficult such a dialogue can be if parents do not speak English:

> The only way I could communicate with the parents was by phone, so I would call and leave a message and the uncle would call back. Now the uncle is gone, but the parents can understand some

English. They always tell me they understand even if they do not, and I am doing cartwheels to make them understand.

Betty and Kathy turn to school social workers and community case workers to learn about bilingual students' backgrounds. Carol recalls how she studied a Chinese child's language and culture:

> Quickly I could see that she loved numbers, and she started show-ing us how she could do math. The mother would come to school often and read to her and the other children in English. She would bring in books that had words and ideas for her child and include other children too.
>
> I then went to work to research this child's culture, what people do, how they eat, how they live. I asked the child to draw what she remembers about her country. Then I spoke to the parent liaison to learn about this child's background.

Most of these teachers also learn about child-rearing practices in various cultures in order to understand behavioral issues that occur with bilingual students in their classrooms. Manuel and Hannah use the library and community resources to accomplish this, but par-ents are the primary resource for most teachers attempting to bet-ter understand child-rearing issues. As Betty explains:

> I just try and talk directly with the parents if it is the behavior thing I am confused about. Among our boys, there are some really pam-pered and spoiled boys who are really used to doing what they want. I learned that it's a sort of an "old world" way of treating your six-year-old like a baby. These kids are bright and come from very caring families who are still dressing them in the morning and giv-ing in to them all the time.
>
> These kids are coming from one child-rearing background of being dependent and then coming to a social situation in our class-room where they are expected to be independent. "No, I am not going to put on your jacket even if you cry," I say.

All the teachers recount stories from families describing how differ-ently children were brought up as boys or as girls, brought up in rural or urban settings, and brought up according to social-class norms. They take on the challenge of studying a child's language and culture because they believe it is vital to their work with both children and families throughout the school year.

Recognize the differences between home and school cultures. All six teachers further suggest that studying the language and culture of the bilingual child enables them to see differences between the child's home and school cultures. Betty describes how she managed to help two children from very different home cultures adapt to the culture of the school:

> I had two children arrive in September . . . very different cases. One was a child from Ethiopia named Heaven, who I later found out was raised in a refugee camp. She came to this country in March with no English. The other, named Vivi, came from Scandinavia, whose father was a visiting scholar from MIT.
>
> I knew nothing about either language. We, for each of them, tried to do things that did not depend totally on language. If we were doing songs, I would make sure they had visual cues or physical movements. If our talk was about a color, I would put out that color marker. For activities in the classroom, I would make sure that myself or one of the adults in the classroom was close by these children trying to make sure that they could get as much out of it as they could.

For Vivi, these modifications were all that was needed, but Heaven still had difficulty adapting to the school culture. Betty worked diligently to understand Heaven's home culture because the child's behavior intimated that her home environment was vastly different from the culture of her school.

> I would always try to talk to one of her parents at the end of the day to let them know what happened. I say to them, this is what I saw the child do, maybe you can find out something and tell me tomorrow. This worked, since the parents really cared a lot.
>
> What worked with Heaven was getting books from different countries to share in class. I remember when I brought some books from Africa: after our sharing came the first word that Heaven said in here, "Africa, Africa!"
>
> When she first came here to the school, she was squatting on the stool in the cafeteria and she was eating with her hands, bread

dipped in ketchup. She would go through six cups of ketchup, and then we finally understood that she thought it was lentils she was eating. We learned that she was very hungry. We had to help her do everything differently in our school.

Each teacher recalls stories of children who had troubles early on with language, social issues, and learning, but who eventually were able to understand class activities and work with other children. Hannah talks about a French speaker from Togo; Kathy recalls a child from Malaysia; Manuel describes a child from Uganda. All six describe various stages of adjustment that they had observed. For example, Hannah says

> Now he will say "book . . . book" instead of gesturing. After a while he is using simple sentences and certainly he understands, since he mouths the words in stories to show us this.

Kathy says

> On the first day his dad left and he was screaming at the top of his lungs. Comforting him and holding him helped. But today I was just saying to him, "Do you remember at the beginning of the year when you never talked and now you can tell us stories at show and tell? It's amazing."

Having carefully watched the second-language acquisition and cultural adjustment process, these teachers know what to expect in terms of language development with a new student. For example, Kathy spent six months observing Fallon, a bilingual Portuguese speaker, and knew that issues of language and culture were not the only reasons she was struggling. Manuel and Kathy note that if a bilingual child is grappling with language and literacy issues for more than six months, they begin to look at the possibility of learning problems. (See Chapters 5 and 6 for their detailed case studies.)

Recognize the cultural transitions and offer support. Individual classrooms have their own "culture," and a bilingual child's success depends on comprehending that classroom culture. Manuel calls the classroom culture "my community of learners"; Carol calls it "knowing the rhythm of my group"; Betty talks about "translating our classroom expectations." Each teacher describes how they initiate children into the classroom community, explaining the rules that govern classroom behavior and the reasons behind them. Parents and other classmates play an important role in this initiation process and offer vital support.

Four teachers rely on another child to initiate a new bilingual student into the classroom culture and encourage that child to facilitate the adjustment of the new student by being a "buddy." Kathy and Carol describe these cultural brokers:

> If it was time for drawing . . . I put them next to someone who was pretty good with that. At meeting time . . . I try to sit them next to somebody helpful, always being aware of where they were, and who they were with.

> After meeting I would ask a child who I know is helpful to pair up with this child . . . to take them by the hand and to show them where the bathroom is . . . where we keep our coats and hats. Sometimes I am lucky and there is a child who speaks the same language as this child. If that were the case, I would pair them immediately and tell them that they can speak any language in my class.

All the teachers indicate that other children are indispensible assistants in the adjustment of a new bilingual student. They believe that peers can translate classroom culture to other children in ways that teachers cannot.

In some cases, teachers create a communication system with parents to facilitate the child's transitions into the classroom culture. Carol tells the story of her work with a Chinese parent:

> Chin-Lu came to us from China. The mother was doing something here—studying? The mother could speak English, but the child could not. The mother came with her the first day and stayed. As we went through the day, she told me what the child may understand and what she would not understand.
>
> She explained to me what activities in the class the child previously had no experience with. The mother showed me what words the child might understand—go, come here, no, pencil—then the mother would go around and tell me the names of things in Chinese and in English. The mother, the child, and I made a system for the very next day.

Integrating bilingual students into a new culture requires a great deal of creativity, and both peers and parents become "cultural brokers" to facilitate the child's transition—into a new environment.

Theme 2: Creating Environments for Language Learning

Although understanding language and cultural issues is important, these teachers note that planning an effective classroom environment for bilingual students is equally crucial in preparing to assess them. The learning environments these teachers create for their students are designed to facilitate learning without knowing English. The teachers use the following methods to plan their classroom environments:

- Organize the physical environment for student interactions.
- Use symbols and cues to translate classroom expectations.
- Provide routines and consistency in daily schedules.
- Create a recording system for observing and assessing.

Organize the physical environment for student interactions. Each teacher admits making conscious choices about the physical environment of their classrooms. These choices facilitate bilingual students' active participation in learning activities while they acquire language skills. Each teacher's classroom design includes a physical layout that allows for multiple observations and assessments of student interactions. Their classrooms foster communication and interaction and provide separate learning areas for individuals and small groups. In every classroom, dividers and tables are used to define separate spaces, each of which is designed for three or four children and contain one table and three or four chairs. (See classroom diagrams in Chapters 5 and 6: Figures 5–1 and 6–1.)

Betty describes the connection between classroom design, student interactions, and informal assessment:

It's the way my room is set up that helps me know about a child. We have our days set up so that for three hour-and-a-half sessions, an adult works with five children. That helps each of us really interact with each of them. Then we rotate and I stay with a group for a week. I get to watch their interactions, and that is how I know what they can do.

Teachers who are close observers of children, like Marina, set up an environment that allows the teacher to pay attention to interactions between small groups of students from any vantage point in the classroom:

> The most important thing is the interaction of that child with other children in the classroom. The bilingual child is going to learn as one child observes the other. It happens while they are working alongside each other. In that interaction is a lot; it's learning in action.
>
> I know that the child starts by being part of the school, part of the classroom. As this happens, he is getting lots of words and he is getting lots of skills. When I feel comfortable with the child in this environment, then it's time for me to start my assessment.

Marina says "in that interaction is a lot," but only when she feels the child is comfortable in the environment does she actually do an assessment. All six teachers observe an individual bilingual student's interactions while working with small groups of children in order to assess their learning over time. Keeping track of observations for each child will allow them to piece together a picture of the whole child later.

Use symbols and cues to translate classroom expectations. Hannah's and Betty's classroom environments clarify classroom expectations and allow children to operate without language barriers. Hannah paints an elaborate picture of the alternative cues available to children in her second-grade classroom:

> There are other means of communication, not solely language. There are posters, charts, pictures . . . pictures of four kids when there are four openings in the listening area.
>
> Children who know little English can walk around the room with another child and sort of get to know where the construction area is, where the writing area is, where the blocks and other things in the class are.
>
> The nature of the work in the classroom will be based on using materials and manipulatives so that every child can participate, because every child can paint, every child can build, use blocks. There is an expectation that there are things this child can do while they are acquiring some proficiencies in English.

In her kindergarten class, Betty has color cues, props, and signals to help children see what to do, even if they cannot understand what she says:

> I just carried on with activities that have cues to help them understand. We would do songs and I would have each line written in a different color. We would be talking about single words, and I would always have a picture to go along with it.

Kathy, Manuel, Hannah, and Carol also have props to facilitate language learning: maps and weather symbols for talking about the daily weather, a pretend microphone for public speaking to classmates, picture cues for job charts and daily activities, and color codes for sorting materials into appropriate storage places. Carol and others use a personal signal system for non-English speakers:

> I encourage all the children to speak clearly to help us all understand, and tell them it is OK to talk to each other in English or in their own language if they want to.
> I always tell any new child that comes into my room that if you do not understand to come to me, tap me on the shoulder, and I will try to tell you again in another way. I am happy to talk with my hands or with a translator, if I can find one.

The environment in each of these classrooms provides many ways of teaching English and communicating with children about daily routines and activities. As Betty says, "Whatever we do, we use manipulatives or cues that help us *see language* and *learn vocabulary*."

Provide routines and consistency in daily schedules. All six teachers have a consistent daily schedule that includes at least two to three hours of literacy instruction. This allows them to prepare many informal assessments. Overall, each teacher devotes at least one-third of the day to literacy activities, with corresponding assessment. As Manuel explains: "Along with a schedule that provides a significant time devoted to literacy instruction, there are small daily assessment activities built into it."

This structure allows teachers to use multiple strategies for instruction and assessment of bilingual children. Betty, a kindergarten teacher, explains her curriculum and built-in assessment activities:

Our literacy lessons help us keep track of how a child is doing. For example, on the 100th day of school we talked about 100, and fixed 100 straws into bunches, and then read *101 Dalmatians.*

I asked them to number 1 through 3 and then I asked them to retell the story in pictures. It tells me about listening skills, interpreting skills, organization, story recall, and motor coordination.

We also work with the children on their journals, and sit and individually talk to them about what they are drawing or writing. . . . I always ask for a family portrait. I look at the details in the drawing, its composition, what it tells me.

The focus on literacy remains a major component of the daily morning routine of instruction and assessment.

Creating a recording system for observing and assessing. Each teacher creates methods for observing skills and recording observations. Marina and Manuel write notes on Post-it stickers and place them in a grid drawn to replicate the activities of their classrooms. These daily notes go into anecdotal records in a file folder they keep on each child. Hannah uses taped conversations, tape recordings of her reflections, and running records:

I tape-record my thoughts and I use very archaic shorthand to take down exactly what the kids say, with abbreviations. I find clipboards to be helpful, and I just section them off so I know that I am taking notes during writing time, during sharing time.

I make notes like "the child would not share with the group but would share with a friend." These kind of affective things are important because as the child starts to feel more safe and secure, you can take more risks in the classroom community.

Betty and Kathy rely mainly on recording observations and keeping running records of students' daily interactions in the classroom. Carol writes notes in her plan book. Both Betty and Kathy observe and document their thoughts, yet each records their ideas differently.

I mostly just write down my thoughts about kids. I take that back— I do systematically record about math labs . . . because math labs, because we are split into groups, is very finite and you can record what you see. We teachers talk constantly and we do journals, so there is writing every day. (Betty)

It is just a lot of observation. . . . I think initially I would try to establish some kind of baseline for where the child starts, and then maybe keep a running record. . . . A lot of times I try, but I do a running record in my head . . . keeping track of what they do in their journals and keeping track of the kinds of stories they produce in writing workshop. (Kathy)

These teachers showed great variety in the formats they utilized for documenting daily observations of their students. Each format fits the context of the particular classroom. Carol and Marina describe developmental checklists they have adapted to compile periodically what they know about individual bilingual children. Kathy also uses an observational checklist developed by the teachers at her school, and is adapting the Work Sampling System, a commercial system for record keeping developed by Meisels (1992), to record observations. (This is part of the Cambridge Schools systemwide reform effort described in the Methodology.)

Thinking and planning before performing classroom assessments is a common theme in all the teachers' stories. They describe using a classroom design, a classroom communication system, a classroom schedule, and a recording system for keeping track of children's ongoing language learning. They study the languages and cultural practices of the children in their classroom, then organize and plan their classroom environment to uncover and develop the strengths of these learners.

Theme 3: Teaching and Learning Is an Interactive Process

The belief that teaching and learning are interactive processes rooted in the social context in which they occur is the major reason why the six teachers assess as they do. While several factors contribute to their assessment methods, they revealed three tenets that, in their words, "guide [their] daily classroom practice and assessment process."

1. Learning is based on building relationships and making connections.
2. Language is best learned in social interactions.
3. Curriculum comes from the interests of the child.

Learning is based on building relationships and making connections. All six of these teachers make personal connections when a bilingual child enters their classroom. Each teacher acknowledges that forming a relationship with a child is vital to teaching him or her. Manuel and Kathy introduce themselves and read a story with the new child. Betty and Marina stand beside the new child and ask questions. Carol interacts with a new bilingual child to begin to build a relationship:

> I first try very hard to hear that child's name and to pronounce it properly. I will be playful with the child and repeat their name until they show me I sound OK.
>
> My main concern is that they are comfortable in the classroom. At the beginning, it may mean keeping the child with me. Beside me, you know; that physical contact is key. They can even hold my hand and look around the room.

Language is learned best in social interactions. Most of these teachers learn about a new bilingual child's language by watching social interactions in the classroom. All six identify a time period in which they observe a child's interactions and watch how the child's first or second language is used. As Kathy, a grade 1/2 teacher, tells it:

> First of all, I would let the child have time to adjust before I did anything. I would just let the child interact with other children and observe. See what kind of interaction I see, see if they work with other children. . . . I would want to let the child have a little time to adjust before I put them on the spot.
>
> I look to see if they are talking to other children, and I see what they choose to do.

Their years of experience with second-language acquisition in children means they can see patterns. All six teachers describe a learning progression with these children: an initial "silent period" when the children observe others; a "mimicking stage" where they copy others; a period when they attempt their own single-word phrases; and, eventually, comprehensible conversation.

Some teachers note that these children speak first to their classmates and then to adults. Kathy has observed the process of language acquisition based on social interactions:

It's amazing how common the steps are in the progression . . . first them just sitting there watching . . . then trying to communicate by pointing . . . and then not really talking very much and understanding then the next step.

They start to talk to peers and to me on a very limited basis—only when they need something or want something. Or, it's an individual conversation and not in front of the group. Then they go on to talking in front of the group—it's really kind of neat. It happens with consistency.

Curriculum comes from the interests of the child. According to interviews, none of these teachers see themselves as controllers of curriculum development in their classrooms. In fact, they indicate that they try to use the children's interests to guide their daily lesson planning. Five teachers have methods for discovering a child's interests. As Kathy explains:

> I would really make an effort, if this child came from a country I did not know very much about, to find out as much as I could about what interests them so that I can incorporate it somehow into the curriculum. Even if it is just for a short time, I teach about their country. . . . In fact, if that child is having some trouble adjusting, then I do it as quickly as possible.

Kathy describes building most of her science curriculum around her students' interest in the neighborhood gardens. These six teachers use an assortment of methods to build units of study or curricular projects from student interests: they interview students, do questionnaires, and have suggestion boxes in their classrooms.

To summarize, these teachers begin with a process of thinking and planning related to the learner and the learning environment. They make a conscious effort to *do better* at assessing bilingual children by clarifying their pedagogical views, by *understanding issues of language and culture,* and, finally, *by creating an environment for learning language.*

UNDERSTAND ISSUES OF LANGUAGE AND CULTURE

Accept and Value the Bilingual Learner

Learn About the Student's Culture and Language
from parents
from community resources
from natives of the culture
procedures as visual cues

Learn About Child-rearing in Other Cultures

Support Process of Cultural Transition
Use a student as a "cultural broker"
Use a parent as a helper in class
Provide, or watch for, a signal to ask for help

CREATE AN ENVIRONMENT FOR LEARNING LANGUAGE

Design Learning Environment for Interactions
Provide spaces for individual, small group, and large group
   interactions
Provide opportunities for teacher observations

Use Symbols to Translate Routines
Give directions that pair physical acts and words
Use charts/pictures/color codes
Provide visual cues as clues to classroom

Provide Routines
Consistent daily schedule
Two to three hours of literacy built into schedule

Develop a Recording System
Teacher anecdotes
Student journals/writing folders
Samples of projects/art
Photos/tape recordings

4

How Teachers Do Classroom Assessments

Noting Struggles and Breakthroughs, Discovering Strengths

Assessment is actually an ongoing kind of thing; *you think about the child and then you do several things,* and teachers that I know each have a different idea about it. There is no cookbook to it, but you need to keep paying attention to what you see, what you see with children and what happens in the classroom

Like Hannah, the other teachers in this study explain that they carry out a "sizing up" process as described by Airasian (1991), which means that they use a variety of informal assessment strategies to guide their instructional planning. A common classroom assessment pattern for these teachers is first to look at the bilingual child individually, then to look at the child in relation to the entire group.

The methods they use to assess the learner suggest a collaboration between teacher and student. Assessment becomes a mutual process of uncovering students' strengths and noting students' daily struggles and breakthroughs. Three strategies cited by a number of early childhood educators are prominent in these teachers' assessment processes.

Kid Watching: Learning about children by watching how they learn

Keeping Track: Collecting raw descriptive data on individual children to be summarized, interpreted, and quantified

Documenting: Observing and collecting evidence of children's learning

Each strategy is woven into the teachers' daily classroom work. Carol, for example, combines "kid watching" and "keeping track" to document the language and literacy of a bilingual child:

> I do my best to learn about a child's language and learning through paying attention to them. Periodically through the day I try to zoom in on them and observe their interactions within the class. I ask myself . . . do they fear adults . . . do they participate in group activities . . . do they play with other children . . . do they follow directions?
>
> I watch and then listen to what they say to see if this child is understanding what is going on—comprehending the language of the classroom. I start making notes about specific skills as they work with others . . . are they picking up the sound–spoken word relationship? . . . Then I make more notes on language and literacy.
>
> I do it—my assessments—more informally, by observing and writing running records of what I see.

Carol's method represents a significant pattern in how these teachers think about, plan, and implement assessments of bilingual students: looking first at social interactions, then at cultural issues, and finally at specific skills in language and literacy.

HOW TEACHERS ASSESS INFORMALLY

Theme 1: Probing an Individual Student's Learning Strengths

The teachers assess each child, bilingual or not, individually. Carol describes her daily routine for assessing the literacy skills of one bilingual child:

> I let the child be center stage with the pointer at some time each day. I look carefully at what they do. I note what they do. . . . Do they follow the words on a chart? . . . Do they read ahead? . . . talk in a loud voice? . . . pronounce the words clearly?

I also use the word charts to songs and to movement games and I ask each of the children to teach these activities. When they are center stage, I take mental notes and most of the time I put these notes in my plan book to guide my plans for the next day.

Betty focuses on assessing an individual bilingual child's oral reading in a similar way:

> When it is their day to read, the child picks a book from the gray box that they really know, and reads or tells the story in front of the class.
> **That for me is a way to see them in action as an individual and when I can tell what they know.**

The following assessment strategies are used to answer questions about what bilingual students *know* and *can do* in language and literacy areas:

- Observe social interactions of teachers and students.
- Question students as they are learning.
- Interview students about their learning.
- Collect student work in a portfolio.

This process allows teachers to pinpoint the way a particular bilingual child learns, and to gather information to test their assessment hypotheses during the course of daily instruction.

Observe social interactions of teachers and students. Each teacher employs a combination of observational skills to investigate a bilingual child's language and learning skills, noting behavior patterns, social interactions, and preferences in classroom activities. Betty describes the observational format she uses for children who do not speak English:

> It's easy in kindergarten. . . . You can watch Heaven, an Ethiopian child, while she plays in the blocks, and you ask yourself, is she making patterns? You can watch her drawings, you see that her figures are easily complete. You can notice when we are singing songs with motions whether she is following directions. You can see whether she follows the pattern of the day. You can see her daily self-help skills.

Yes, it's a lot of observation, you can even watch what she is doing in the water table. Is she making connections with other children?

Betty focuses on Heaven's visual, motor, perceptual, social, and auditory skills in order to assess her strengths. Similarly, Marina observes and documents individual bilingual students' daily progress by focusing mainly on language and literacy areas:

> I watch a child more closely when they are developing language skills in English. For this assessment, observation is basic. I may observe that the child likes to draw in September, and then I see that he knows how to write his name, first and last, by November. I keep track of these and I am on top of their literacy learning.

All six teachers observe daily interactions related to:

1. teacher-student interactions;
2. student-student interactions;
3. student-materials interactions.

They cite specific interactions with bilingual children in which they assess language skills, as in this example from Kathy:

> I do not think I do a formal assessment of language. I really do not do that with children who are not English speaking. I think I just sort of talk with this child, you know, just read a story and see if the child is somehow able to communicate the story back to me. That kind of thing . . . very informal . . . very nonthreatening. I do this periodically to check up on how this child is learning language and understanding.

Carol similarly describes her interaction with a child who spoke no English:

> Well, I tell you what I did with a little Chinese girl. When she did not understand what to do, she would tap me on the shoulder, and I would tell her again . . . this is what I did.
>
> I do not really assess language as much as I try to *give language to the child* and see if they can work on it with me first and then even see if they use that language with the other children.

Carol touches on a key point: "I try to *give language* to the child and *see if they can use it,*" the implication being that if a bilingual student can *use language,* then the natural process of acquiring English will unfold.

Carol and the other five teachers display a keen understanding of sociocultural theory, which assumes that language is embedded in the social interactions between teacher and students, and of students with each other. Although they use individual methods to observe the social interactions of bilingual children, they all consistently focus on how bilingual children *use language* by looking at their gestures and their drawings, then recording what they say. Betty describes her interactions with Heaven:

> We would be talking about single words and I would always have a picture to go along with it. I made sure that when I spoke to her, I would use one idea at a time. I found that we first would communicate through touch, and then through drawing, until we could use single words.

Sometimes the teachers enlist the support of the native English speakers in their classrooms to collect information about the bilingual students with whom they work. In three of the second-grade classrooms, a system of paired reading is used. In paired reading, students first read with a buddy, then are asked to assess each other, using a chart to give their "buddy" a written assessment (see Figure 4–1). Hannah, in her grade 1/2 class, has native English speakers and bilingual children give her oral and written feedback about each other's language and literacy skills.

> I rely strongly on children as experts . . . and as peer resources. Kids say to me . . . did you see her read a book today? . . . or . . . did you see him learn this letter today? . . . because they are working alongside this child.
>
> When you put children in charge of themselves and each other, it is cooperative and it is problem solving. I have kids walking around with clipboards and monitoring what they are doing, monitoring their group activity . . . and they are in charge of everyone else's participation.

Second-grade teacher Manuel, pairs children for daily practice in oral reading in an activity he calls *pair-share reading,* and shows them

Name _____   *PEER ASSESSMENT*
                                         PAIRED READING
Title _____

Author _____

Read to Self   M   T   W   Th   F

Read to a friend   M   T   W   Th   F

Friend's Signature _____

Read to a teacher   M   T   W   Th   F

Teacher's Signature _____

Title _____

Author _____

Read to Self   M   T   W   Th   F

Read to a friend   M   T   W   Th   F

Friend's Signature _____

Read to a teacher   M   T   W   Th   F

Teacher's Signature _____

Figure 4–1 *Sample Peer Assessment Paired Reading Form*

how to give each other feedback on what they read. In her kindergarten, Betty pairs children to assess and teach each other during
daily alphabet activities.

It was when . . . we had finished our alphabet books, they worked
in pairs. . . . They had to trade alphabet books . . . look through
their partner's book and pick out the three best letters. Then they

had a piece of paper where they had to write the three letters that they picked and then go to the cover of the book and copy the child's name on their paper. They actually did it all.

All these teachers have bilingual students and their classmates assess and teach each other language and literacy skills. Four out of the six teachers ask native English-speaking students to fill out a form that asks questions about their classmates' language and literacy skills. The other two teachers have students assess each other orally during group meetings or by looking at samples of their peers' work.

Question students as they are learning. All six teachers question or interview students to keep track of what they are learning in their classes. This means watching what the children do and asking them what they are doing—questioning them and listening to their responses in the course of daily literacy activities. The teachers spend from three to five minutes every day questioning each child. They do this by circulating through the classroom, questioning bilingual students as they read in pairs or write in their journals. A specific time for this daily activity is usually set by the teachers, and varies in each classroom.

This questioning format is another way for teachers to "size up" bilingual students' language and literacy skills for instructional purposes. The following exchange between Hannah and Gino, a bilingual student, illustrates the guided questioning that she uses to assess his decoding strategies for reading:

> GINO (*Struggling to read the book* The Scientist): I cannot do this.
> HANNAH: Then what do you do when you do not know a word?
> GINO: Look for clues . . . in the pictures. . . . I looked.
> HANNAH: So what else can you do? How about looking at the whole sentence?
> GINO: It goes like this . . . (*He reads*). . . . I am not sure.
> HANNAH: Does it make sense to you?
> GINO: Yes, but here I'm not sure. (*Pointing to words that are unknown*)
> HANNAH: Look at this word and this word . . . they are hard words and you read them correctly. Can you tell me what it says to you then?

Hannah's specific questions assess Gino's decoding strategies, an important literacy skill. Manuel uses a similar series of questions to gather information about a bilingual child, which then becomes the basis for his informal assessment of the child's language and literacy development:

> I want to know what this child knows . . . what letters he might know and what he does when I give dictation. What happens when we try to label things in the room? . . . I ask them . . . "What do we call this?" and I listen for what that child says.
>
> I then go on to see what happens with the child when they handle books. I look to see if they can predict, do they have a sense of meaning when they read. I do this as I listen to them read me a story, and after, I might ask them to tell me what happened to see how they can interpret meaning from what they read.

Betty's questions accompanied by focused observations are part of her informal classroom assessment:

> I am watching and listening to our interactions when we work together at the tables. I record what I recall in our conversations, and what I see in work samples and in details of writing.
>
> I try to slow down and see what the child does and ask them to tell me about it.
>
> I have most of their work in little books and I date it. I know that with Heaven I could see that she was using more vocabulary each day, and I tried to note it and then she just burst into phrases.

The methods of observation are a means of keeping track daily of their bilingual students, and the raw descriptive data they collect tells the story of each child's progress in language and literacy.

Interview students about their classroom experience. Teachers sometimes use guided questioning or interviewing as an assessment tool. Marina individually interviews each of her bilingual students to find out what they know and what interests them in the classroom.

> MARINA: Which activity do you like in the classroom?
> STUDENT: Reading, writing, drawing, games.
> MARINA: Which activities do you find difficult?
> STUDENT: It is difficult for me to sit in group.

MARINA: If you have the opportunity to choose any activity in your classroom, which one do you choose?

STUDENT: Toys and puzzles.

MARINA: Which part of the school do you like?

STUDENT: Singing, reading, and playing with my friends.

MARINA: Is there something in the classroom that bothers you?

STUDENT: Oh, painting. . . . I do not like painting . . . and I do not like housekeeping.

MARINA: When you are mad what do you do?

STUDENT: When I am angry . . . bammm!

She uses what she learns during these interviews to design a curriculum that responds to what her bilingual students want to learn.

When a bilingual child is particularly puzzling, the teachers interview parents, other school staff, and other children in the class to gain more insight into the child. Interviews with members of the student's home culture and school culture can reveal the child's strengths in each environment. Interviewing parents helps Betty in the early stages of language assessment, and also helps her deal with a bilingual child who may be frustrated by not understanding what is occurring in the classroom:

> We watch her body language a lot and then ask other people about it. . . . With Vivi, things would happen, like if there was a change in the schedule . . . she would all of a sudden start crying and we did not know why and it could have been anything.
>
> I would always try to talk to the parents at the end of that day to tell them what happened and ask them if they could find out something and tell me tomorrow. . . . This works. . . . The parents talk to the child and to me and it works. The parents care.

As Betty suggests, combining student and parent interviews helps give the teacher more information about what a child is learning, how a child is learning, and what the teacher can do to facilitate that process.

Develop student portfolios. Each of the six teachers also has a method for collecting student work into a portfolio. The formats are customized to the particular classroom, school teaching teams, and activities that occur each year in the school community. Marina describes her collection process in detail:

Oh, we all work with the portfolio system. Here is what I do. I have a big folder and a small folder. There is a portfolio for each child and in it I put what the child does, which are books, small books, their journal, and sometimes a favorite picture of the child.

Sometimes I sit with the child and pick what should go in and sometimes the child picks. You see that in the portfolio are some examples of writing, not all of our work.

The work has dates . . . see, January . . . February. I introduce this collection of writing in January, and all the kindergarten teachers in the school are doing this. Now, one time each year, we go through the portfolios of children together.

We have this portfolio review meeting with the child. Each meeting focuses on a subject . . . on reading or on writing. In the portfolio are samples of art, writing, math, and other pieces . . . and then I interview the child to listen to what they tell me about their work.

Marina and the other kindergarten teachers in her school have a system for selecting items with students for their portfolio and then reviewing the portfolio contents with the student, other teachers, and the child's parents.

Hannah's students include tape recordings of oral reading as well as artwork and writing samples in their portfolio. They include samples of all types of art, and often try to include some form of dramatic retelling related to familiar stories used in the class. Betty organizes her kindergarten students' portfolios in a similar way:

I say to the children, "We have a file box and we keep our work." In this box there are self-portraits, four times a year, four picture stories. I tell them that I want to keep their three best letters and then I go to the copy machine and I copy the piece they select, and here it is.

This is the kind of record keeping I do . . . and when you combine a portfolio of student work with your own journal writing on the child . . . it gives a "richer" understanding of that child.

Kathy describes her portfolio system as a collection of children's work, which has specific components:

I am preserving one story that is considered their best story from writing workshop, one per month. Those are dated. I am keeping their journals and what I do is xerox important milestones that show their progress. I also keep what they write in their math journals. Then I take photos of their constructions and their projects so I have a record of what they did and what they said about it.

Carol's student portfolios follow a format designed by primary teachers as part of their coordinated learning project:

> I keep folders . . . I keep samples of handwriting . . . drawing . . . artwork . . . I date it. . . . Look on the walls to . . . see what the children did in October. . . . Now look here in the portfolio. . . . I also have them do journals. . . . Here is Jon's book in the portfolio . . . in the beginning he was doing simple drawings . . . now, in May, look at the drawings—they are more elaborate . . . they have a story to them. . . . I write the story here and now Jon's starting to put his own letters in the corner. . . . These are samples of the children's portfolios. . . . They tell me a lot.

Manuel's portfolio system contains a recorded questioning process, a collection of student work, and conversations with the student:

> Mostly I collect samples of the child's work. . . . I keep a portfolio of their writing, and this to me is data about the child. I look at the samples and when they happen. And then I sit down with the child. I listen to what they say about their work.
>
> It's their feedback about their work . . . what they are telling me that is important. From the students' portfolios, I am collecting ongoing ideas about what this child is thinking about and enjoying in the class and what I should think about teaching.

According to these teachers, each student portfolio contains evidence of ongoing and authentic student learning (Wolf 1989) related to daily classroom activities. Marina sums it up:

> I like interviews to ask students questions, portfolios to look at student work . . . and my own observations. It gives you so many things. This is my assessment. . . . This is it for me and this helps me help them learn.

LINKING ASSESSMENT AND INSTRUCTION

Theme 2: Monitoring Ongoing Interactions While Assessing and Teaching

All six teachers assess and teach bilingual students as part of their ongoing daily classroom interactions utilizing the practices listed here:

- Observe student's language and literacy over time.
- Analyze student's learning process.
- Reflect on observations and student's work.
- Create a mental file on each child.

Observe student's language and literacy over time. Teachers document skill development in language and literacy by focusing their observations on specific instructional activities. Manuel relates a typical assessment of a bilingual student:

> I want to know what the child knows . . . what letters he might know . . . what does he do if I give dictation . . . what happens when we try to label things in the room . . . I ask, what do we call this? I see what happens with the child when they handle books.
> I am looking to create success . . . can they predict . . . do they have a sense of the meaning? . . . All of this is when they listen to a story. . . . I ask questions about stories, saying, what happened after that?

Kindergarten teachers in this study consistently focus more on language development, and grade 1/2 teachers more on literacy development. Marina, a bilingual kindergarten teacher, directs her language assessment format toward social interactions and the bilingual student's process of cultural adjustment:

> I think that to give an assessment of that child's language skills, the most important thing is what we see in interaction of that child with other children. The learning process is not only confined to the evaluating done by me.

One child observes the other at work . . . one child learns along-side the other. . . . To give a good assessment, I have to wait a long time and watch what kind of behavior comes from that child . . . when I feel sure that this child is adjusted, I write about what I see.

I record my impression of their learning interactions. To give time to that child to make friendships first and then observe. In that interaction a lot is there. It's a process . . . it's related and it is a part of his/her adjustment. I know that for children from other cultures that come to us, it's first being a part of the school . . . it's being part of the classroom, then it's what am I supposed to learn.

Hannah and Manuel are more interested in assessing literacy learning in order to comply with what the school system's expectations of second-grade students. Hannah's approach to assessment is geared accordingly:

I use Marie Clay's *Concept About Print* [a structured conversation around reading] as documentation for the system.

I sort of adapted it, since some of the procedures were too much. I do not need to do all that counting of words the child misses.

I keep ongoing records and look at a *child's writing samples,* writing across the content areas, so that I keep all of their writing.

Art and *play* are strong indicators because the bilingual children are able to express or retell stories through a mural, a play, or painting a picture. That for me indicates comprehension and cog-nition, so that art is often where I see them translating ideas.

Dramatic play is extremely effective for all children, but especially second-language learners, since in this way they have the opportu-nity to make a statement. I gather some ideas from all of these pieces to get a picture of the whole child.

This process examines language and literacy skills through writing, drama, and art. Hannah and other teachers combine informal techniques with system-driven assessments to compare bilingual students to others at that grade level.

Analyze student's learning process. Manuel takes note of a bilingual student in the classroom over time, interacting with that student on specific learning tasks.

I think this sounds funny . . . but what I have is a sort of recipe in my head. I first look at the *child's interests* . . . what is known and unknown to this child.

Then I look at *what happens when I give the child nudges* . . . when I tell them something new to move them on to new interests.

Then I look at *how they react to the environment* . . . what I see as far as hands-on experiences . . . I want to know what the child does with these types of activities.

Oh yes, *book handling* . . . how does the child approach books . . . look at them, use them . . . make them. . . . Then, I am big with *dictation*. . . . I have each child *keeping a journal* . . . and all written work goes in there.

I actually have a journal of my own on children and I write little anecdotes about the child. The only other thing I do is a Miscue Analysis of their reading at the beginning and end of the year to study the errors they make when they read.

Kindergarten teacher Carol lets the child take the lead while she teaches:

In the shared reading, I let each child have a chance to be center stage with the pointer each day. I look carefully at what they do. I note what they do.

I also have charts of songs and movement games and I ask the children to each lead these activities and see if they read the words. When they are center stage, I take mental notes . . . and most of the time, I put them in my plan book. . . . They guide my plans.

Carol recalls how she noted in her plan book what Somni, a bilingual child, could do and used that information to tailor her teaching:

Say, for example, Somni is saying the beginning of words and not the endings. . . . I will try to include more activities for her to do with me or in the group and see if I can work on that [ending sound skill] with her.

Reflect on student work. Manuel evaluates bilingual students' literacy learning by reflecting on student work:

Mostly I collect samples of their work. I keep a portfolio of the child's writing. This to me is data about a kid. I look at other work samples and think back to when they happened. I listen to what the child says about the work, which I think is direct feedback about learning. I really look at their published stories . . . they are in their writing folders. Those really are what I look at.

I am also using the *"keeping track"* records . . . which are a sort of note on a grid. . . . It has Monday to Friday written on it. . . . I write down what we do here [he shows me a grid]. It's marked "sharing" . . . "listening" . . . "paired reading" . . . "book talk" . . . "concentration." I put little notes to myself on the grid when I can to remind me what they did and how I see them change.

How and where these six teachers collect information reflects the context of their individual classrooms. Variations in their approaches are most noticeable in their recording formats.

Create a "mental file" of student learning. Hannah uses a "mental file" to guide her teaching, building on the children's interests:

What we are doing now—having a conversation and tape recording—that is what I do with the kids, and I listen to these during dinner, especially with kids I am really concerned about. I have records on every child, but the child that I am trying to document is progressing and I try to develop curriculum around what they are learning, what they know and what they need, and that is where my time is spent.

Carol's reflections indicate that she values how two girls who spoke no English relate to each other as they adapt to daily classroom life:

I can tell that they have a stockpile of information because they nod appropriately, and do activities and artwork that shows that they understand.

I see that they are always touching each other and they relate to other girls in the class by stroking and smiling at them.

The classroom assessment process for these teachers is an ongoing, active, organic process involving observing, questioning, interviewing, recording, collecting, reflecting, and assessing. In the next two

STRATEGIES	TECHNIQUES

Kid Watching
learning about children by
  watching
	observing daily interactions
	recording observations
	using checklists and running
	  records

Keeping Track
collecting descriptive data
  on individuals
	questioning students about
	  their work
	interviewing students and
	  parents
	conferencing with students
	  and teachers around port-
	  folios

Documenting
observing and collecting
  evidence of children's
  learning
	teacher narrative summaries
	student portfolios of sample
	  work
	tape recordings of oral read-
	  ing
	Reading Miscue Analysis
	  (Goodman)
	Concepts About Print (Clay)

chapters, I turn to Kathy and Manuel to provide detailed accounts of their daily classroom assessment. Kathy is a monolingual teacher who, like many veterans in today's teaching force, has developed strategies from a combination of inservice training and school-level initiatives. Manuel, a bilingual and bicultural teaching veteran, has personally experienced language and cultural transitions, and so has worked on his assessment process as a teacher of diverse learners.

Kathy and Manuel each have twenty years' experience in dealing with diverse learners and have reflected on their practice in an ongoing documentation and assessment teacher study group. Although each teacher has unique strategies, both see learning as an interaction, which supports the idea that assessment involves looking carefully at the learner and the learning environment.

5

Portrait of Kathy
Kids Helping Kids

The first portrait of practice is Kathy's. As a monolingual teacher, she is representative of most educators in today's American classrooms. She was trained as a teacher and special educator in the 1970s at a teachers college where a behavioral approach to literacy focused on decoding and achieving measurable goals and objectives. In 1985, she joined the Cambridge Schools Literacy Project, led by Don Holdaway, and became a member of the documentation and assessment study group. For nine years, she has been revising her classroom practices, focusing on multiple formats for curriculum and assessment as part of inclusive programming for bilingual and special education students.

Kathy, at age thirty-nine, has bright blue eyes that sparkle as she talks about her professional life. For the last six years, she has been a primary teacher at the Harrington School in Cambridge, Massachusetts. She is about five feet three inches tall, has wavy, jet-black hair, and looks younger than her years. Her slight frame and dancerlike carriage give her the appearance of quiet assurance as she circulates the perimeter of her classroom. As she walks, she is smiling and checking on each of her students, asking questions or listening to comments. She often engages in conversation with a child, chuckling in response to what she hears. She obviously delights in the funny things that young children say and do.

Kathy has adapted her teaching to a sociocultural framework for classroom assessment of bilingual students. She is keenly aware of issues of language and cultural transition, although she works only in English. She is unable to carry out assessments in the child's native language or interview parents without the help of a translator. Ideally she would like to develop better skills in understanding language acquisition and in surveying home language skills. She realizes that she has a limited knowledge of what her bilingual students know and can do, and relies on other specialists—the bilingual school psychologist and early childhood specialist—to supplement her classroom assessment work. She also works as a coteacher with Liz, a Spanish and Portuguese speaker who provides additional expertise to the teaching team.

Kathy, a former special educator, and Liz, an early childhood educator, coteach an integrated grade 1/2 program. This classroom is considered "integrated" because it serves students from many linguistic and cultural backgrounds, some with special education needs. This year Kathy has sixteen students in all, six of whom are identified as having special education needs.

Her classroom environment communicates her fundamental philosophy of teaching and learning—that learning is a cooperative activity done alongside others. Upon entering her classroom, one quickly notices that *kids are helping kids*. This philosophy guides how Kathy thinks about and plans to informally assess bilingual children.

BACKGROUND, LANGUAGE, AND CULTURE

Kathy proudly explains that she is a product of the Cambridge Public Schools and has been a teacher in the school system for the past eighteen years. She is also a member of the strong Irish Catholic community of Cambridge, historically a driving force in city politics and in the schools. She laughingly recalls early days as a teacher in Cambridge, when she was working alongside people who had been *her* teachers. Now she too is meeting some of her first students who have become teachers, and so the cycle continues.

In informal interviews, she revealed that she did her undergraduate teacher training at Lesley College, also located in Cambridge.

She was certified in special education, which was at the forefront of educational reform in the early 1970s. As she recalls:

> You knew if you were trained in special education you would always find a job, and I found that there were so many exciting new ways of serving different and challenging children. I wanted to be a part of that movement.

Kathy has continued to take courses, looking for innovative ways to serve special needs. Although trained to serve special needs students outside of regular settings, she now prefers "mainstreamed" classrooms that allow these students to learn along with "more typical" students.

Like all special educators in Cambridge, Kathy was trained to teach reading using a phonetically based decoding system called the Gillingham Approach. After years of experimentation with several approaches to literacy teaching, she adapted a whole language approach, which includes systematic presentation of phonetic skills in context. As she explains, "I now see that decoding skills need to be taught in context, while reading real stories, so that children understand what they are doing and why they are doing it. Sometimes I ask parents to share in word games and word play to help link language and literacy development to the home."

Kathy has worked with both elementary and high school students in regular and special needs programs. Over the years, she has found that she has more enthusiasm for young children, who are still motivated to learn:

> When I first came to this class from a special education [SPED] "self-contained" class, I was hesitant to work with young children again because I had not done it for a while. Now, I find that I enjoy working with this very mixed group of young children. You know, in September, the SPED kids and their issues really stand out from the others. But now, in May, I see that this class has really come together as a group. Maybe it is the "set up" of our classroom. I see they all made a lot of growth.

At this point in her career, Kathy has experimented enough to know what works for "challenging" learners. The remainder of this story describes how Kathy thinks about bilingual students, plans their classroom environment, and informally assesses their language and literacy skills.

UNDERSTANDING ISSUES OF LANGUAGE AND CULTURE

Specific practices help Kathy and other teachers understand the language and culture of bilingual students. Chapters 3 and 4 listed a variety of teaching practices and strategies used by the six teachers in the study. Kathy's interpretation of these common practices shows her creativity and ingenuity, and emphasizes the fact that teaching strategies, in order to be effective, must be customized to the individual's needs.

A Philosophy of Teaching and Learning

Kathy's philosophy of teaching and learning is rooted in direct experience:

> When a bilingual child comes to me with a big SPED folder, I read it and sort of put it over there . . . but I guess I learn in the same way that these children do . . . from "hands-on" experience. I find out so much more by *being with the child* than I could from what I read about them on paper.

She accepts and values each child's learning differences, especially those related to language and culture, because of her premise that *any* child *can learn,* given an environment of consistency, support, and encouragement. Kathy values her students' background and culture as she talks about the bilingual students she serves:

> There is great acceptance of individual differences in this room . . . different cultures and languages are here, like with Carlos, Ruth, Fallon, Elias. We have someone from a different country or with a different learning style . . . special needs . . . physical . . . emotional . . . speech . . . It is all part of who we are.

Three premises form the basis of her pedagogical approach:

1. Direct experience is a key element in curriculum development.
2. Kids learn by helping other kids.
3. Parents are vital partners in the child's learning process.

These ideas are apparent in Kathy's reflections and plans and in her classroom environment.

Children's Interests Are Key to the Curriculum

When Kathy discusses curriculum, she considers herself the classroom "choreographer" of themes that come from the children's background, interests, and ideas. Questions that children ask are the catalyst for what is studied. In Kathy's classroom, children constantly talk, read, and write with one another in every activity they do. Kathy combines their input to create lessons that integrate science, art, and writing:

> *5/19/94 (science observation)*—This activity stems from a Portuguese parent's donation of earthworms and kids' interests in knowing more about them. Children work in pairs, recording their observations and measuring worms. They are adding new vocabulary . . . worms have bristles . . . their bodies are in segments. Now they are estimating the worms' length using their pencils and unifix cubes like rulers. Finally, children work on reading their earthworm books together with their teacher. As they read they are recording information about their observations of worms.

Literacy learning is *the* primary focus in all Kathy's classroom activities, including math and science.

Parents as Partners in Learning

Parents are involved in the daily life of Kathy's classroom and play an active role in numerous classroom activities: offering ideas for classroom activities, gathering curricular materials, and reading aloud with children. Parent volunteers help teachers tape-record samples of children's oral reading. On Thursdays, one parent takes individual children to read storybooks and records this event with a cassette player. The tapes are collected, marked, and kept in binders so that children have evidence of how they "sound" when they read aloud.

Parents are also Kathy's partners in creating weekly curricular themes in science and art:

> *5/22/94 (science observation)*—One parent who likes to fish sent in worms, which were the impetus for a unit on earthworms and their natural habitats. A second parent came in three days later and

made an earthworm "treat" with small groups of children. Using a plastic bucket and shovel, she made and then mixed chocolate pudding and Oreo cookies, which became the "earth." Then she added candy gummy worms, which children buried in the "earth" using a shovel. This cooking and construction all packed in a bucket was then refrigerated and served for afternoon snack.

Over the next few days, reading the recipe and comparing observations of the "real" worms' habitat and the "candy" worms' habitat became a follow-up science activity for Kathy's students. Since bilingual parents have reasons to come to school regularly, Kathy has many opportunities to gather important information about children's cultural background and family lives.

Kids Helping Kids

Kathy's fundamental teaching goal is for children to be active participants in the teaching and learning process for themselves and for their peers. This is particularly helpful when pairing children as "Reading Buddies," because it often means that when there are significant differences in learning and language abilities, one child's strengths will bolster another's weaknesses.

> In this room, the SPED kids really help each other, as well as encourage their peers a lot. . . . Even Jonathan, who really does not read but is a native English speaker, says to other children who are learning English what he hears us saying to them. He says . . . "sing it out when you read" . . . he means "sound it out" . . . even though he cannot necessarily do it himself. The reminders they give each other are also what they hear back from each other. . . . It keeps them trying harder.

Kathy has organized her classroom program so that kids can help kids to understand expectations throughout the day. Children read, write, ask each other questions, and provide each other with ongoing feedback about their reading and writing progress.

CREATING ENVIRONMENTS FOR LEARNING LANGUAGE

Kathy's classroom environment and related curricular and assessment practices are the structures that support her sociocultural process for classroom assessment of bilingual students. Planning the environment and activities carefully is crucial to successful and accurate assessment.

Creating Environments for Learning Language

- organize the physical environment for student interactions
- use symbols and cues to translate classroom expectations
- provide routine and consistency in daily schedules
- create a recording system for observing and assessing

Organize the Physical Environment for Student Interactions

The physical space of Kathy's classroom reflects her philosophy of teaching and learning. The space is designed for kids to help kids and for parents to work as partners in small and large group activities. The overall plan provides places for teachers and parents to work with small groups of children (see Figure 5-1).

The classroom layout includes seven separate work spaces where teachers can work with pairs of children and be physically separated at tables so they can concentrate on reading without distractions. The design allows writing to go on at three tables in one area. Since Kathy is close to these tables, she monitors most of the students' work simultaneously. The rug area where children sit and talk to each other is a focal point of group discussion. Their conversations with teachers center on what will happen, what did happen, and what they learn. Large group meetings occur periodically during the day: after journal time, after the snack, after choice time, and during Shared Reading.

Use Symbols and Cues to Translate Classroom Expectations

The classroom environment is full of symbols and charts that help translate what goes on each day in Kathy's classroom. On the walls are charts of songs, poems, and chants as well as reminders of classroom procedures and skills. Each activity in the daily schedule has a chart or prop to go with it. For example, the daily schedule is posted on an easel, the morning activities use a weather chart, the Reading Buddies activity has a step-by-step procedure chart, and Writing Workshop has a chart that outlines the steps of the writing process.

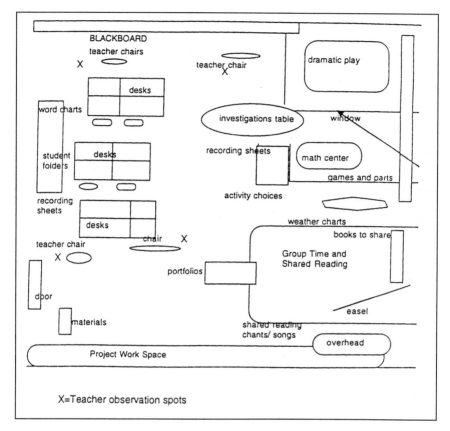

BLACKBOARD
teacher chairs

X ⬭

teacher chair
X

dramatic play

desks

word charts

investigations table

window

student folders

desks

recording sheets

math center

games and parts

recording sheets

activity choices

desks

weather charts

books to share

teacher chair

chair X

X ⬭

Group Time and Shared Reading

portfolios

door

easel

materials

shared reading chants/ songs

overhead

Project Work Space

X=Teacher observation spots

Figure 5–1 *Kathy's and Liz's Classroom*

Symbols and charts serve as reminders and reinforcements for students learning language. Charts of most of the commonly used sight words (known as the Dolch list) decorate a clothesline that hangs across the room. Children use these charts throughout the day to help them with reading and spelling activities. Symbols of daily activities using picture cues help students see their schedule.

A Schedule of the Day

Although most of the morning is devoted to literacy learning, specific activities focus on individual skill development. Essentially the same set of routines follow each morning:

7:40–8:00	Sign-up/Journals
8:00–8:45	Writing Workshop
8:45–9:45	Reading Buddies
9:45–10:00	Snack
10:00–11:00	Math/Language Activities
11:00–11:45	Choice Time
11:45–12:15	Shared Reading

During activity time, children spend twenty minutes on math and then choose from projects involving writing, computers, or art. Four children each select one project. Kathy and Liz are careful that children do not always choose the same activity. In most activities, the teachers are moving around, spending five to ten minutes with each child. They help each child start to read or write by talking about ideas, asking probing questions, and guiding the child to completion in a step-by-step fashion.

Create a Recording System for Observing and Assessing

Kathy and Liz have developed a recording system for keeping track of each student's daily literacy learning, which includes writing folders, written Reading Buddies response sheets, audiotapes of oral reading, home reading book lists, and journal pages:

- We collect Journal Pages and the Reading Buddies sheets in a ringed binder . . . in chronological order.
- The Portfolio is another part, which includes bimonthly self-portraits, artwork, and some favorite math papers. Children choose what they want in the portfolios.
- Then there are samples and notes from Writing Workshop, which means that on the folders of student writing, we write anecdotes about what we observe or learn as children are in the act of writing. We make sure that one observation of writing behavior on each child is recorded each month.
- There is the Progress Report in the binder, which is a composite developmental checklist of skills . . . from Meisel's Work Sampling . . . which we record on each child. Under each developmentally based skill area are categories indicating skills that . . . are developed . . . are developing . . . are not observed . . . and we check one of these.
- This collection of information goes into the binder. We have this

binder of documentation that gets passed on to the next year's teachers, and the portfolio that is for the child and the parents.

In Kathy's recording system, each curriculum activity has an explicit written assessment component built in. The children are responsible for much of the record keeping and for compiling papers into binders. This alleviates some of the teachers' daily management problems.

Kathy's informal assessment format is based on gathering student work and teachers' comments as descriptive data both on the process and the products of children's learning (Engel 1990). (*The Cambridge Documentation Handbook* [Engel 1995] provides additional examples of formats for "keeping track" of student learning.)

LINKING ASSESSMENT TO INSTRUCTION

The methods Kathy uses to assess—to *"sit beside the learner"*—indicate that she sees herself working with students in a joint process of investigation. Her practice, like that of others in this study, is a process of uncovering students' strengths and noting their daily trials and triumphs. As she describes:

> I look at what they do each period every day. I ask myself, "How do they write their name when we have daily sign-in sheets? What are they doing in their journal entry? . . . Are they just drawing or are they writing?"
>
> During Reading Buddies time, I learn about what stories they read and what strategies they use for reading. . . . I see if they use phonics skills. Reading Buddies is when I have that individual time with a child at the table. It lets me see whether a child knows the sound-symbol relationship and lets me hear what they understand.
>
> Also, I get additional information during Shared Reading time. We look at how the child responds when we mask certain letters in words from the text . . . we observe if they can recognize a letter from their name . . . a letter from our word cards. These things really let me know where they are at in literacy areas . . . I find that I learn much more than I did with any individual testing.

Specific activities that are part of Kathy's daily classroom program link assessment with instruction for individual bilingual children.

Journal Time

Journal time allows Kathy to interact daily with individual bilingual children and keep abreast of what is meaningful to them. Each morning children are asked to write something they are thinking about. They are given an $8\frac{1}{2}$-by-11-inch sheet of paper divided in two, with the top half left blank for an illustration and the bottom half lined for a written description of the picture (see Figure 5-2). Each child has about thirty minutes to draw and write about their thoughts. In most cases, children write about their families and daily life at home.

A typical journal-time interaction is depicted in Kathy's exchange with Elias, a Greek-speaking child in her classroom:

KATHY: How is your story coming?
ELIAS: I need help.
KATHY: OK. Let's start with just one idea and write it down.
ELIAS: My grandfather has sheep on his farm in Greece?
KATHY: OK. How do we start . . . write "MY". . . just start with the beginning.

This child does not know the sound-symbol relationship, so Kathy brings out an alphabet card so he can find a picture as a cue to the first letter of the word. Kathy has him trying to sound out the words "my" and "Grandpa." He writes the first word slowly with her help, and then she writes "has a lot of sheep." Elias continues, "I like the black one." They work together on the remainder of his story. She writes his ideas down, which he then copies on his journal page.

Journal Assessments

During journal time, Kathy asks her students questions like "What is happening here?" in order to better understand the children's backgrounds and family life. In the example above, Kathy observes Elias's drawing and asks questions in order to find out what he is trying to write about. Although he can tell stories about his Greek background, he struggles and cannot find the appropriate words in English. He has difficulty remembering the sound-symbol relationship in English, which makes it difficult to generate writing without assistance from a teacher or another student. Kathy has observed that even with picture cues, he cannot consistently match the correct sound to the letter. Decoding is strenuous for him, and he can only try to sound out two

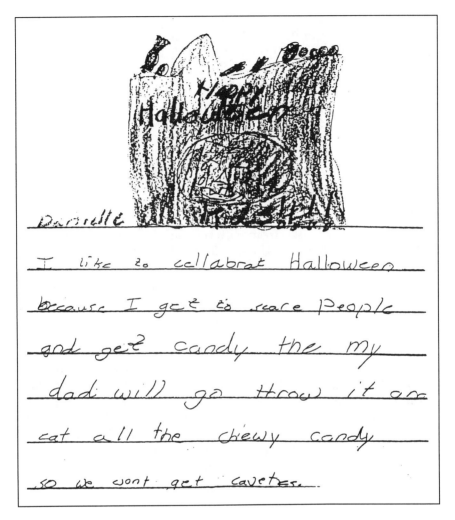

Figure 5–2 *Journal Sample*

or three words at a time. For this reason, he needs her to translate his thoughts to paper, so he dictates his journal entry and later copies it.

Reading Buddies

For about thirty to forty-five minutes each morning, interactive reading takes place between pairs of children. The theme of this activity, like the theme of Kathy's practice, is "kids helping kids."

Strong readers are paired with weaker readers. The children begin by getting their reading folder, in which they have their current reading book and a log of books read. Also in their folder are other reading aids, such as alphabet charts and common word lists. A chart on the wall explains the process:

---

1. Read to a partner.
2. Listen to a partner.
3. Fill out a reading form.
4. Read to the teacher.
5. Write a response.
6. Practice your book on the rug.

Children choose books from different levels, which are in color-coded buckets so the teacher can keep track of their reading progress.

Children read and talk about their books, then fill out their record sheet with their buddy, and then with the teacher. These record sheets keep track of the pages read, the challenging words, and the child's responses to what they read (see Figure 5-3).

When children have trouble recording information, their buddies may fill out the sheet for them. Ruth, a Persian student and a strong reader, fills out Jonathan's sheet for him every day, while other children do it themselves. Children who struggle with spelling copy from the book cover and text and record the title and author's name on their record sheet. Each day children file their record sheets into their binder, keeping them in chronological order. After the children have read to each other, one member of the pair reads with the teacher. As Kathy explains:

> You know that Reading Buddies, as we called it, started as an experiment to avoid reading groups because Liz and I both did not want to do them. Children and their buddies read aloud to each other and we then watch and listen to them after they practice this way.

When Kathy or Liz checks in with individuals, she listens, assesses their skills, and then helps them with specific decoding and comprehension strategies. In a sense, the teachers are observing and informally assessing bilingual children during Reading Buddies to see what meaning they derive from the text. Kathy demonstrates this as she works with Randy on *Mag the Magnificent:*

READING BUDDIES

NAME:_____

TITLE:_____

AUTHOR:_____

Reading Buddy:_____

Read to a Teacher:_____ DATE:_____

Keep the same book   Get a new book

_____

_____

RESPONSE:

_____

_____

_____

Figure 5–3 *Journal Sample*

5/22/94 (classroom observation)—As he reads the first three pages, she checks to see if he understands the word *asparagus*: "Do you ever eat asparagus like he does in the story or have you tried them before?" Next, Randy is stuck on the word *giant*, and Kathy says, "Look at the last three letters." He sees *ant* and looks at the picture and says "giant." Randy later struggles to read the words *Magical Indian Suit,* and Kathy stops him. "Look at the picture," she says.

"What does he have on?" Now listen to those words . . . you hear
how many syllables, like we talked about this morning. . . . Clap
them for me.

This is an example of that "teachable moment" when the
teacher makes connections with an earlier minilesson on syllables,
and she checks to see what the child remembers.

During Reading Buddies, Kathy and Liz monitor five to six children
so that each gets daily personal attention. They seem to interact for
four to six minutes per child, reading, discussing, and recording.
More time is spent with those who struggle to read.

While Kathy reads with bilingual children daily, she is observing
and making notes about specific reading skills.

I look at fluency . . . miscues . . . challenging words . . . all of these
skills are recorded on the lines provided on Reading Buddy sheets.
The children's breakthroughs, when they discover a pattern or
strategy, are recorded. For those working on chapter books, I note
which page the child has completed. I record whether they go on
to a new book or stay with the one they have. After listening to a
story, I pose a question for the child to write about in response to
what they read.

The following example describes the interaction between two students and Kathy; one is a strong reader and one is struggling:

5/22/94 (classroom observation) [Kathy reading with Paul from
Brazil]—Look here, you just said the word *cannot* and some letters
are missing. For this we say *can't*. This is a contraction, so let's look
for other contractions in our reading . . . [They go on reading and
point to contractions]

As I listen I am going to write two words on your sheet, which
are *says* and *should* . . . you need to practice these. . . . OK? I am
writing this on your sheet so that the next teacher who reads, you
check on these words again.

[Kathy, reading with Jonathan] Haven't you read that book? I think
that I heard it. [They do go back to check the cover sheet where
finished books are logged . . . a checklist of all the books according to
reading level is taped to the pocket of the folder.] We need to keep
track of what we read . . . here Jonathan . . . we read this book. Let's

find a new one [he is a struggling reader . . . he repeatedly avoids reading harder books and brings out those that he knows].

There is an obvious rhythm and spirit in the Reading Buddies period. Bilingual children who are beginning readers, like Katie, Fallon, and Elias, are proud to read their little books to any adults who enter. They all seem to feel like they *can* read, despite the recognized differences in their abilities. Some children are reading books with chapters while others are reading books with three to four lines on a page. The structure and organization of this activity gives Kathy a daily opportunity to assess her students and informally gather ideas about how to teach them more effectively.

Reading Word Cards

Parents asked Kathy and Liz for a word-game activity to do with their children, and the teachers responded. Every night, children are assigned to practice reading word cards at home with their parents to foster home-school relationships. During Shared Reading time, the teacher checks on these sight-word cards by reading them with the child. The cards have two-inch printed words from the Dolch list of most frequently used words. Each child has a pencil box for the word cards, which have a hole punched in them and are attached on binder rings. The teacher holds the master word list and marks whether the child knows the word or not. When a child has mastered the assigned words, the teacher gives him or her three more cards, which are added to the child's box of word cards on the ring. The accumulated cards provide visual evidence to the bilingual child and to his or her parents of the child's improvement in recognizing sight words. (This sight-word assessment is part of the Work Sampling procedures currently being piloted by Sam Meisels at the Harrington School.)

Preparing for Parent Conferences

Before Kathy and Liz have a conference with parents about a child's progress, they review the pieces of information they have gathered over time. Conferences take place in November and May in the Cambridge schools. On the day of a parent conference, Liz showed me how she prepared Carlos's portfolio. She explained that she and Kathy made a joint decision that one teacher take the lead in compiling a single child's work into a portfolio package. SPED children's portfolio records and reports are Kathy's job. For other children, Liz assembles the following documentation:

• Reading Buddies record samples— May, April, March, October	4 pages
• Journal samples— May, April, March, October	4 pages
• Writing Workshop— May, April, March, October	4 pages
• Audiotapes of story reading— May, October	
• Personal/social development 4 self-portraits, May, April, March, October	4 pages
• Math—4 worksheets with comments on addition, subtraction, concepts	4 pages
• Progress report—composite of all areas	3 pages
• Portfolio work with art, science, math samples— children choose	3 pages

I watched Kathy quickly organize information into a professional, comprehensive portfolio of selected data on a child. After examining the student's work, she wrote a narrative on the child that was added at the end of the progress report as a summary of the student growth over a three-month period.

MONITORING INDIVIDUALS WHILE TEACHING AND ASSESSING GROUPS

Kathy monitors individual students while assessing and teaching small groups.

> Again, to assess language, I focus on what I observe happening in the classroom. I want to know how that child is understanding what goes on. When we are on the rug, how is the child following directions . . . how does the child listen and respond to stories?

How do they express themselves, how do they participate in group time, in classroom activities? I guess what I want to know is, can that child make themselves understood, and can that child understand what is happening in the class?

During morning activities, one child is "center stage" for a week, which means that the child gets an opportunity to stand before the group and tell about the calendar, the weather, and the daily class schedule. The following is an excerpt from Kathy's field notes:

> *5/19/94 (classroom observation)*—This week is Katia's turn to do the calendar. She puts the date card in a packet, and says, "Today is Thursday, May 19th, 1994." Next she acts like the weatherman, holds an imaginary microphone, and predicts today's weather. She says . . . "today is sunny and cold" . . . then she takes stickers representing these weather conditions and places them on a chart near Massachusetts on the map of the U. S. Then, using a map as a prop, she tells the class about the weather and places representative symbols of clouds, rain, or sun in certain parts of the U. S. . . . in Texas . . . in Florida . . . in Canada . . . in California . . . and in New York.

Kathy takes mental notes twice a day in order to analyze an individual bilingual student's learning process and reflect on that student's work. She uses Shared Reading and Writing Workshop to focus on the individual in relation to the group and to analyze students' progress.

Shared Reading

During Shared Reading, children read aloud to the whole group, which is seated in the rug area. The teacher begins the activity with a coffee can filled with poker chips bearing each child's name. The teacher draws a name from the can, and that person gets to read something of his or her choice to the group. After they finish, they ask, "Are there any questions or comments?" Three children are allowed to raise their hands to give feedback to the reader. When individuals ask for questions or comments from their peers, most often they receive compliments about their reading. The following classroom observation captures this process:

5/22/94 (classroom observation)—Kathy, in order to observe, chose her own name from the coffee can and decided to read a big book to the group. She chose to read *Mrs. Muddle Mud Puddle,* which is a story about an old lady who got confused trying to find her house because she did not wear her eyeglasses. She engages the children in reading the text, pointing with a pointer, and intermittently asks questions.

"Joe, can you read the title for me? Katie, who is the author? Randy, what do you think will happen in this story?" Pointing to the illustration of the old lady, she continues, "What is she doing here, Elias? Try to guess why she does these things. Ruth?" She reads three pages of text and asks the group: "Now, can someone tell me more about her? What do you know now? . . . Why is she mixed up?"

After assessing that they do understand the story, since they have successfully answered her questions, she finishes this book and asks for any questions or comments. Two children compliment Ruth and Elias for helping them understand the story.

During the next Shared Reading, she monitors Paul's understanding of reading while she is teaching and assessing:

5/23/94 (classroom observation)—"Now look at this page . . . what do you see?" [She refers to the quotation marks she told him about earlier.] "What do they mean?" . . . Paul says that he thinks that they mean someone is talking. "Yes Paul," she says, "they mean that someone is talking and this is what they said. Where else do you see these?"

Other children respond and notice the quotation marks and begin to read what is inside the quotes as dialogue between different people by changing their voice tones.

Kathy repeats this simultaneous assessing and teaching process with word attack skills. When she came to the word *sure* in the text, she asks, "What does this word say?" Ruth answers "sure." "What is the sound at the beginning?" "Sh," they all call out. Kathy then remarks to the group, "So here is one of those words we cannot sound out, which we have to learn by looking and remembering . . . just like the words on our cards."

As Kathy later said in her informal interview, "I do not do 'Gillingham Method' any more . . . but I still do bring in those skills for him when it is time . . . when they are ready and when they are faced with a need to learn them from a text. The teaching of skills is done in the midst of the Shared Reading process so it often has meaning for them."

Children reflect on their work in several ways during Shared Reading activities. Sometimes children have a chance to share their audiotapes of oral reading with their classmates. Using a cassette player, they play the tape of their October reading and then their May reading. Their progress in oral reading is obvious both to themselves and to their peers.

During Shared Reading activities, children read their writing to the group and then reflect on their work. In this example, Elias's name is picked, so he shares his journal story:

> *5/23/94 (narrative summary)*—Elias reads aloud his story about "Sheep in Greece" that he wrote during journal time. After he finishes reading, he asks his classmates if there are any questions or comments in response to his story.
>
> Children raise their hands and one asks, "Why do you like to write about Greece?" Another asks, "Why do you like to speak Greek?" He answers them, explaining that for him to learn Greek means that he can have friends in Greece when he goes there to visit his grandmother and grandfather. In a sense he is reflecting on his personal writing themes and explaining them more clearly.

Throughout each day, children demonstrate growth in language and literacy skills to their teachers and classmates. At the same time, Kathy and Liz are assessing what these children know and helping them reflect on what they have learned.

Writing Workshop

Once a week, the Early Childhood Resource Specialist joins Kathy and Liz to run an activity called Writing Workshop. Each of the three adults works with groups of four or five students talking about and then writing about their daily lives. Field notes describe the interactions in Writing Workshop:

> *5/23/94 (classroom observation)*—In this activity, five children are seated at each table and one teacher is at each table. The Early Childhood Resource Specialist is the third member of the teaching team for this

activity. Each child has a folder for Writing Workshop. It contains writing samples, dated, and charts to help with spelling. The prewriters have alphabet cards, some with picture cues if needed. Those that are able to sound out words and letters get a dictionary.

Charts in the room offer printed examples of common sight words. Words come from frequent usage lists, as well as ongoing science and math study.

On the back of the folders are stickers with teacher anecdotal records. Each sticker has a note about what strikes the teacher about that child. It seems that notes are written in cursive and dated, which means that children cannot read them. Two written anecdotes on each child are visible each month.

Kathy and the other teachers use this time to informally assess their bilingual students. This observation describes Writing Workshop one Monday in May:

> As I watch, Kathy is working with Elias as he struggles to tell and then write about his favorite animals in Greece. She wrote the following on a sticker and placed it on his folder: "Elias 5/94 knew symbol for H/h and with visual cues, b, l, a, s, c. He knows that there are periods at the end." She is helping him use his alphabet card to sound out letters to write words.

At other times, Kathy asks calculated questions to help direct students' attention to what they write. She says, "Tell me about this word. Look here . . . what does it say on the page? Read it back." This is part of the editing process. At this point in the year, Kathy feels she can focus the children's attention on grammar and usage and not just fluency. Writing Workshop is a time when children help each other spell as they write, read drafts of their writing, and give feedback to their peers.

Throughout each day of classroom life and during each activity, Kathy is linking assessment information to instruction and looking for ways children apply their literacy skills to other subject areas.

Creating a Mental File on Each Bilingual Student

Kathy's teaching methods allow her to create a mental file of her bilingual students' progress. The following story illustrates how she uses a "mental file" on Fallon to distinguish the child's learning problems from language acquisition issues:

The child that comes to mind is Fallon . . . because she has issues beyond being bilingual . . . like auditory processing issues, sequencing. . . . Well, she came to us with a lot of testing and I read it and sort of put it [aside]. . . I find out so much more by being with the child than I could with what I read on paper.

Sometimes I get really frustrated because progress is slow, and that is when collecting all these little pieces shows me that she is making progress. . . .

I tried all types of strategies for reading and I found that she really had some visual strengths . . . visual memory is one. I could then see what she can do by collecting all these little bits of information, these little assessments. This is really what I find helpful.

I know by sitting beside her that she can match letters and sounds, although she cannot remember the name of the letter. While teaching her I found that if I give a sound to her, she can identify the letter. Yes, she is making progress. I think that the set up of the room really helped us with her; because we have two teachers, we were able to try different strategies.

Now we are recommending that she go to a smaller language-based classroom. Although I think we do a lot of language in this classroom, she is still a puzzle to some extent. I think that she has benefited by being here . . . being with positive role models.

Her confidence is strong . . . and I see that she knows when she doesn't know what she should know. Sometimes she gets anxious, she wants to respond and she can't. She knows what to do about it now, she uses her resources, so she will find a friend to help her, a book to copy from. I see she knows where to look in the classroom to get help . . . she copies from a chart or anywhere she can see a word.

Fallon was in a bilingual class before, and when I went to observe her I saw her trying to write the letter g on the line. I asked her what she was doing, and she told me that she was doing her numbers 10 times on a line. I know that she knows the concepts, but does not fully understand distinctions in symbols and what they mean.

CONCLUSIONS

Kathy is a careful observer and recorder of children's learning activities. She uses multiple formats for recording daily interactions, which determine what she learns about the children in her class. She combines her informal assessments with information from her coteacher, Liz, as well as from parents and other children. Parents give feedback on a child's progress as they help tape-record individual children's oral reading. Children assess each other by filling out peer assessment sheets while they read with each other.

Kathy is the primary force behind the daily classroom assessment of bilingual children. Her assessment and instruction involve kid watching and keeping track of what she learns about her students. Each of the strategies Kathy uses in her classroom is an integral part of her philosophy of teaching. As she concludes:

> I usually find that I want to observe the child during our daily activities. There is not always a single way I choose to do this, but I watch how the child fits into the routine of our classroom. *I keep track of what I see, and it helps me learn about who they are and what they can do.*

Assessment Strategies	Classroom Activities
Kid watching learning about children by watching	• observing daily interactions • recording using checklists • noting in reading/writing workshop
Keeping track collecting descriptive data on individual	• questioning students about their work • collecting journal pages, reading records • taping oral reading samples • interviewing students and parents • conferencing with students and parents around portfolios
Documenting observing and collecting evidence of children's learning	• writing teacher narrative summaries • keeping portfolios of sample work • taping oral reading quarterly • compiling a binder with samples of journal pages, reading records, monthly self-portraits

6

Portrait of Manuel
Creating Lifelong Learners

Unlike most teachers, Manuel understands the process of language and cultural transition into American schooling because he experienced it himself. He is a bilingual, bicultural individual who still struggles with speaking and writing in English. Manuel came to the Cambridge Public Schools having completed teacher training in another country, so he brings a different perspective to his work with children. Manuel firmly believes in "sitting beside" learners to find their strengths, and has designed a classroom environment around this idea.

Manuel is of medium build, a dark-haired, brown-eyed man of forty-seven with a tan complexion. His most striking feature is his wide grin, which appears every time he sees a young child. In his second-grade classroom at the Fletcher School, he is frequently seated next to one of his young students, chatting animatedly. Although he wears glasses, his bright, sensitive eyes and playful facial expressions are a clue to his energetic interpersonal style—a style that is reflected in his view that teaching and learning are primarily personal interactions.

I always want to have a balance of thinking and doing as I work with young children. I go back to my idea of ownership of the learning process for the child. I always believe that children learn best when they know the subject and you, the teacher, show that you care about what they care about. When they write about something they know about and they care about, you tap into their inner thoughts and somehow you get better results . . . not to mention the friendship that goes along with it.

Observing Manuel, one is struck by how deftly he combines being a teacher, a learner, and a friend to his students. His high level of interest and caring for children is obvious in the respectful way he treats all his students. This is shown in the little notes he writes to each child in their daily journals. Reflecting on his work, Manuel describes his mission to create lifelong learners:

I want to help a child learn about or understand how to be a better person. That is, how to at least know what to do to solve problems, and knowing when to ask your friend if you needed some help. These are monumental steps in the learning process.

His sense of urgency and commitment is echoed in his thoughts:

But we do not look at these things consistently through our schooling life. . . . It would be wonderful if we could bring all the kids along this way and help them to understand that education is a nonstop adventure . . . a road to an active and fulfilling life.

His goal as a classroom teacher is to be a catalyst for children, unlocking the many talents they have and bringing those talents alive in a school setting. He encourages his students to invest in their own learning:

The curiosity they have should be used in school. That means that I would like to get around to all of them . . . making myself available to encourage that curiosity. I have to come to them, not them come to me. I believe that it's a real good practice when I do that . . . when I respond to their deep questions.

Manuel is clear that his role as teacher is not to transfer what he knows to his students, but to let them drive their own learning:

I think that my role as teacher is very simple. I always think that if I
spend too much time talking, I take the focus away from them.
Kids will do that . . . if you make them focus on your questions,
then you take the focus away from them and their questions get
lost. When you just kind of leave them with a question in their
head, you're giving them back some lead.

Over the course of his work with the Literacy Project as a whole language teacher, Manuel has experimented with many forms of
instruction and assessment of diverse learners. It has taken him
years to develop strategies for observing, keeping track, and documenting the work of individuals and groups in his classroom. In his
classroom, language and literacy are both work and play.

BACKGROUND, LANGUAGE, AND CULTURE

Manuel is a bilingual Philippine American who has been teaching
for twenty-three years in the Cambridge Public Schools. He is mar-
ried and has two children. Although he is not an outspoken person,
he is someone who has reflected a great deal on the "art and craft
of teaching."

In 1990–1991 he became a Lucretia Crocker Fellow for the State
of Massachusetts for his pioneer work with whole language teaching. He talks joyfully about taking a one-year sabbatical and travel-
ing throughout the state of Massachusetts to talk to teachers about
whole language teaching and adapting a whole language model of
literacy learning for diverse students.

A PHILOSOPHY OF TEACHING AND LEARNING

Manuel's background and culture contribute to his philosophy of
teaching and learning. In his transition to living in the United
States, he found that being able to speak, read, and write English is
vital to being a productive citizen. Manuel feels that he must make
the most of the one year he has with his students to help them develop a love of learning and a strong foundation in literacy skills.

What I believe about teaching contributes to everything I do in my
classroom, so I need to tell you about what I think about teaching.
I focus almost totally on reading. To learn, you need to read, and
it is the key to all subjects. To be a reader you need to make a

thousand mistakes and accept those mistakes. I expect that learners use their mistakes to take new risks, so as a teacher I let the mistakes go for a time in the interest of gaining fluency with language.

His focus on literacy learning transforms his philosophy of teaching
and learning into reality.

UNDERSTANDING ISSUES OF LANGUAGE AND CULTURE

Manuel sees himself as a teacher who shows his students that he
respects everyone's language and literacy abilities:

> You know, it is an acceptance process . . . I wait, no matter how
> long, and say just take your time.
>   That child can sense that I will wait for him and that is impor-
> tant in letting that second-language child know that I took the time
> to wait and that I know they can contribute something.

He acknowledges that he is a second-language learner and therefore has special empathy with students who struggle with English:

> I think that they know that I am a second-language person. They
> know that I am like them. Anyway, it helps. It makes me sensitively
> understand where they are coming from and then build them up
> from what they know. Of course I have met with the parents
> before, and this gives me a good sense of what I need to know
> more about and what I do not have to do. I think a lot of it is
> acceptance and valuing of that child so he can learn.

Manuel is quick to point out that the classroom curriculum itself
must accept and value the learners in the class:

> I think the curriculum has something to do with this, it has to be a
> level that you can reach them and there is an understanding. They
> can see that it is manageable for all of them.
>   But here, with those types of kids like Manauris and George who
> are struggling . . . how I wish that I could speak all the languages
> that they are speaking to help them move quicker through the
> process.

Manuel is eager to study the individual student and he tries to design his teaching craft around that pursuit.

> In the very beginning, I always want to create a story for each one of them. I find something that every child can succeed at . . . from the very start . . . and that is sort of like establishing a foundation. From the very start this helps in knowing how you are going to move this child along. When they start doing the journal, this really starts telling me what I have to do, either on expressive writing or on even the simple conventions. From the journal I learn about their families, their joys, and their fears, which is critical to making a connection with them.

In Manuel's classroom, children celebrate their many languages and cultures in informal discussions. They use their first languages with Manuel and their classmates playfully. Children feel safe to share their struggles with learning language. During an observation visit, the children noticed that I have a Greek name and asked if I could speak Greek to George, who was struggling with a writing assignment. In Greek, George asked me to help explain the work to him and to tell him if he was doing it correctly. Other children, hearing this exchange, asked to learn some Greek words, and conversations about home languages and school languages started. After this, George admitted that he did not understand all the English instructions given in the classroom. Other children who speak Portuguese, Spanish, and Korean told Manuel that this happens to them, too. Then Dalissa said, "Just ask someone to explain it again, because you can get it better the second time." This was a breakthrough for George, and an opportunity for Manuel to acknowledge the confusion that second-language issues sometimes create for many children in the class.

Given the many backgrounds of the children Manuel works with, he feels that he must bridge the differences between home and school culture. He openly teaches about other cultures in literacy activities by sharing multicultural stories and songs and linking them to the personal lives of his students.

Manuel is keenly aware that he must support students' transition into his classroom culture, especially those from bilingual backgrounds. He begins by interacting with the new student individually, then gradually introducing the child to others in the class.

I start by conferencing with the new child and introducing myself and letting the child know that I want him to be comfortable. I often ask the child if there is a book in the room that they want to show me. I ask the child to show me that book and tell me what makes them want it. I ask the child to start off with one child and talk about having a friend. Having someone to talk to, a friend . . . this is what we do in this class.

He wants children to be comfortable in their classroom community and consistently communicates this message. The children often work in pairs, with one child becoming the cultural broker for another bilingual child, explaining what to do in each activity.

Manuel helps bilingual children *learn how to learn* by giving them a set of mottoes to guide them in their "nonstop adventure in learning" and to help them take ownership of their learning:

1. Trying is right, and this is how we learn.
2. To be a good reader takes time and very much practice.
3. In all activities we need to have choices to direct our own learning.
4. We learn from the feedback of others, and by listening to others.
5. When we finish a task we should think, how can I improve this and where can this lead me?

CREATING ENVIRONMENTS FOR LEARNING LANGUAGE

Manuel's classroom space and organization, like Kathy's, reflect his philosophy of teaching and learning. Since his goal is to create a community of learners, he believes that the spaces that children occupy should be small communal areas where "individual possessions" and "boundaries" do not curtail the interactions.

I am trying to do something about the physical space in this classroom. When each child has a separate desk, they cannot help but be worrying about their own property instead of shared property. I really want to create a sense of community in this room and a sense that the things we share and take care of are done together. If I had my choice I would have no desks, but a table and chairs, adult chairs, too, so they can feel big.

Each morning, Manuel circulates almost instinctively among the desks as part of his process of checking in on each child's reading and writing. The regular "visits" allow him to size up each child's daily written work. When he stops to look at student work, he questions the child about his or her work, pointing out areas for editing or suggesting a next step in writing. He is sizing up each child's language and literacy skills for instructional purposes, which means that he is using what he learns by looking at student work to guide his next step in teaching. He questions why a child does what he does or writes what she writes. In essence, he is scaffolding the child's learning process by asking frequent questions.

The physical layout of the classroom includes six areas, each of which accommodates a different type of activity (see Figure 6-1). He frequently moves the children into different spaces when he moves into particular literacy activities. He focuses children on their tasks by keeping them in small, contained spaces. For instructional sessions, he clusters the desks in groups of four. Talking and interacting within small groups is encouraged unless otherwise announced. When he introduces hands-on projects using art and found materials, he asks his students to move to spaces with large tables for spreading out the work.

Manuel is observing children wherever they go in the classroom. Observational vantage points are carefully laid out in his classroom plan, and include strategically placed "teacher chairs," where he can sit and help one child while observing several others.

Manuel actively engages children in learning through his quick but routine interactions with them. He walks past their desks to check on what they are doing. He stands beside them to help them focus on improvement. His main form of interaction involves questioning them about what they do and why they do it.

Manuel's physical presence throughout the morning literacy program seems to keep children working, as long as he is close by. When he is working with one child in a group of six, the entire group of six children stay involved in their work. The children who are farther away seem to work, chat with friends, and then work again. Overall, the presence of their teacher helps keep students consistently engaged in literacy activities.

Symbols and Cues

Manuel's classroom is adorned with signs and pictures that help children remember what happens each day, and where materials are

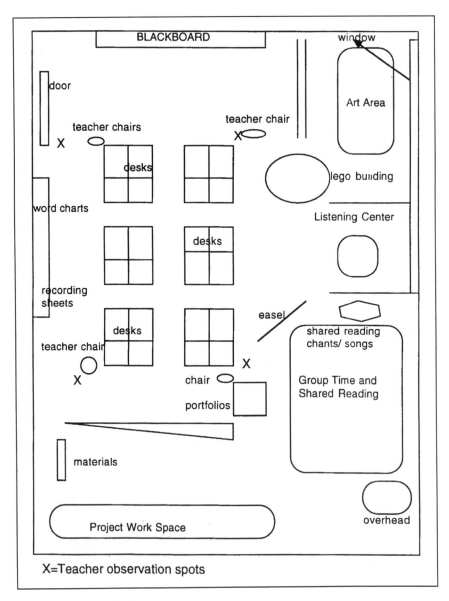

Figure 6–1 *Manuel's Classroom*

stored. He has name cards posted on a chart that tell children with
whom they read each day, and where their reading books should be

placed. His daily schedule is regularly written on the front chalkboard. Pictures, also posted on the chalkboard, give clues about new things that may be occurring (e.g., visitors, special cooking projects, school assemblies). Translating charts, pictures, and written symbols posted in the room are part of daily morning routines.

Each work area in his classroom is labeled with signs that pair words with pictures—Creative Arts, Building Blocks, Writing Folders, Shared Reading and Meeting Area, Science and Math Tables, Work Tables, Listening Center, and Building Area. In Manuel's classroom, pictures and symbols signal what is planned and what is expected.

Routines and Daily Schedules

The way Manuel structures his academic schedule allows him to focus most of his attention on his students' literacy skills through reading, writing, spelling, and other activities. From 8:45 to 12:00, children are involved with reading and writing, individually, in pairs, and in a large group. He gives a lot of time to reading and writing. The schedule below helps explain how each day is structured in Manuel's class:

8:30–9:15	Journal
9:15–9:35	Minder
9:35–10:30	Paired Reading
10:30–11:15	Shared Reading
11:15–11:45	Writing

The morning schedule rarely changes, so children know the routine and can predict what they will work on. Manuel uses routines to keep students motivated and engaged in literacy learning. Students stay motivated by following a schedule that includes a new activity every twenty to twenty-five minutes. As they change activities, they often move into different seats. Manuel describes his classroom environment, commenting on his use of time and the tone of the room:

Time: Since I value reading, I allow lots of time for it in my daily schedule. My day is really built around lots of practice reading. If you focus on paper and pencil tasks or worksheets, you are never engaging in interactions. Reading practice is the main ongoing activity between myself and the children, using many different formats each day.

Tone: The tone of the room helps guide the learning process every day. I start with a quiet mode, focused on reflection in journals and in the minder activity. Then I see that the activity increases during Paired and Shared Reading. Then I work on pulling them back so they remain focused on reading and writing.

Manuel's routines offer consistency and support to his bilingual students and, in fact, to all his students.

Keeping Track

Manuel is able to assess children during the course of small and large group instruction. He describes his method of observing and recording what he learns about individual students:

To do this I have a sort of recipe in my head. I first look at the child's interests . . . what is known and unknown to this child.

Then I look at what happens when I give the child nudges . . . when I tell them something new to move them on to new interests.

Then I look at how they react to the environment . . . what I see as far as hands-on experiences. . . . I want to know what the child does with these types of activities.

Oh yes, book handling: how does the child approach books . . . look at them, use them . . . make them?

Then, I am big with dictation. . . . I have each child keep a journal . . . and all written work goes in there. I actually have a journal of my own on each child, and I write little anecdotes about that child.

The only other thing I do is a Reading Miscue Analysis, where I read with a child alone at the beginning and at the end of the year to have a sample of their skill level.

I really look at the "keeping track" records, which are a sort of noting system on a grid. It has Monday to Friday written on it. I write down what we do [he shows me the grid]. It's marked Sharing, Listening, Paired Reading, Book Talk, Concentration. Then I put little notes to myself about the child on the grid using Post-its when I can.

Manuel has a complex system of record keeping, which he combines with student work samples gathered into a portfolio. Manuel reviews student portfolios with them every two months, and writes summaries of their conversations for each marking period (November, March, and May). The combination of the teacher observations and student work samples provide comprehensive evidence of the process and the products of bilingual students' learning in his class.

PROBING INDIVIDUALS' LEARNING STRENGTHS

In order to determine a bilingual child's language and literacy skills, Manuel follows a "mental recipe," which begins by focusing on social interactions, then systematically observing and recording information during the literacy activities during journal time, minder, Paired Reading, and Shared Reading. During each of these activities, he gathers information on a different aspect of student learning.

Journal Writing

Manuel begins each day with journal writing. These journals, done in English and with pictures, allow children to express their thoughts (Figure 6–2). He explains that journal writing offers bilingual students opportunities to focus on writing, personal expression, and the invention of ideas:

> In the beginning of each day I ask children to write about what they are thinking about. Sometimes I am very concrete and I give them a prompt, like, "It's very cold today," and I ask them to write at least fifty words before they can stop.
>
> As they are writing, I circulate and I make them aware that I am observing and reading their work. Then I try to write a line or so back to them.
>
> I want them to feel a sense of ownership in their work and pride in their writing and share it publicly with their classmates. Then I ask them to share their writing, so I do not mark up their papers. I merely ask them a question and they rewrite to respond to that idea.
>
> I find a way to entice them to revise writing by asking thought-provoking questions.

In essence, he asks children to draw on their prior knowledge of words and grammar to find and correct their own errors. Commenting on the students' evident progress in a journal over time, he says:

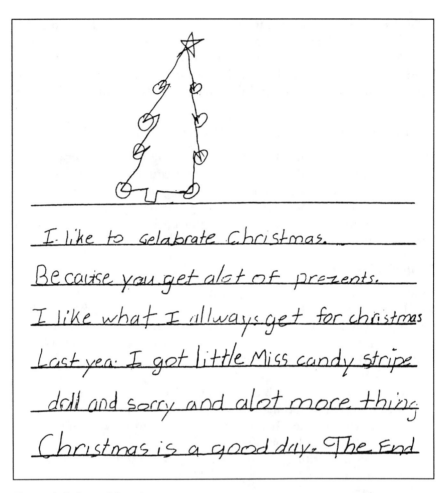

I like to Gelabrate Christmas.

Be cause you get alot of prezents.

I like what I allways get for christmas

Last yea. I got little Miss candy stripe

doll and sorry and alot more thing

Christmas is a good day. The End

Figure 6–2 *Journal Sample*

I think that it is really a developmental thing that you too can see
. . . as they take the next step, when they begin to understand the
next piece. And, even though I am pushing hard, if they are not
ready to think about it or to work on bigger pieces, it probably will
not happen. For me that's a big question. I think that it is better to
approach it all at their level . . . so that they can conceptualize your
message at that point.

Sometimes I think they need to be stretched, though. This is
when I write them a longer note.

He describes specific cases to illustrate his process of linking assessment to instruction for bilingual students:

> With Linton this morning . . . when I read it [his journal], I had no intention of doing this lesson on quotations to help Linton finish writing his play. I always go back and say to myself, do not teach anything because you will have to wait for something else to happen before you can really understand.
>
> You need to teach it during that *teachable moment,* when you can do it. Waiting for that teachable moment is always on my mind and it just happens. I can never tell you when that teachable moment is ever there. From your assessment of what they are asking about, you can see what you need to teach.

He moves around the desks as the children write to check each one by asking them two or three questions. His assessment of the children affects the length of time he spends with them. He spends five to eight minutes with Patrick, George, and Manauris, who need extra help, and moves those who are distracted to a different area of the room. This happened on three occasions with Patrick and Manauris, who were moved to spaces outside the group of desks so they could concentrate on their writing work.

When Manuel looks at his students' work, he determines what to focus his teaching on. He is explicit in what he says to children, and uses their writing as the springboard to new learning. One day, he taught a minilesson on short vowels and on the use of the articles *a* and *an,* in response to Rena's journal entry. He does these mini-lessons during journal and minder time, which focuses the class on learning new spelling patterns and punctuation, taking material directly from students' errors.

He is able to assess or size up ten children in thirty minutes. He notes that in the students' journals they write about the mishaps of their lives—for example, when Patrick's fish got sick, when Rena's mom went to the hospital, when Demetra had a stomachache. Checking in daily keeps him abreast of their important personal concerns that affect their schoolwork.

Minder Activity

In the minder activity, Manuel asks children to reflect on issues in their lives at home and at school. One day he asks them to think about why they do journal writing every day; the next day, he asks them to describe why they have celebrations at home. In each case, children write what comes to mind and then complete their story with an illustration.

Manuel also spends about two to three minutes with each child during the minder activity, when he is actually interviewing them about what they wrote. He reads with each student, asks some questions about what they have read, and offers them ideas to think about. Evidence that he is informally assessing their learning process is apparent in the regular feedback he gives children He specifically notes changes in spelling and reading fluency, and often asks students to explain why this occurs. In his own words,

> I always want to have a balance . . . when I give them this minder activity to think about. In every piece of writing, I think they have a question in the back of their mind. Why am I writing this? . . . Who am I writing this for? . . . I think that they have to acknowledge in their mind they are writing for me because I want them to be a better writer.
>
> They write their ideas in response to a question. My success with the minder activity is because it is so open-ended that you cannot have a wrong answer. They might write only a line for a response to the daily question that I ask . . . and that is OK, I let it go. It is evidence of their day—their feelings and how they are approaching learning that day. Sometimes, before writing, they drop pencils and have to get up and sharpen their pencils. That is part of the whole writing process—getting an idea and getting it down.

Manuel finds that this is the time he can best look at *how* children learn and what new skills he sees emerging.

Collecting Student Work into a Portfolio

Manuel keeps track of student progress by collecting work samples in a portfolio. These portfolios are collections of work that children select to record their growth in literacy areas. He describes student portfolios as the evidence of what they care about and are learning.

For Manuel, the student portfolio is one part of the documentation that he keeps and shares with parents and other teachers. His recorded observations and notes on daily activities add to this collection of work and contribute to the overall picture of a specific child's language and literacy progress.

MONITORING INDIVIDUALS WHILE ASSESSING AND TEACHING GROUPS

Paired Reading

Manuel uses the Paired Reading activity to investigate children's reading strengths and to assess their literacy skills. As he describes:

> First, I ask one child to pick out a book that they can read from cover to cover and they read it with me. I look at how they handle books . . . what level book they choose.
>
> I tell them that I just want to hear them read, and what I observe is that those who are good readers will be willing to take risks. In most cases I see they will be 90 percent right, and try to read a hard book. Then, to assess how they read I look for strategies they use when they do not know a word. I ask them, "What do you do when a word does not make sense as you are reading?" During this time I also remind them of three strategies to use as a reader:
>
> 1. If a word does not make sense, stop, look at it carefully, cover the word, look at the first letter, and guess what word would make sense.
> 2. Reread the sentence and try to see what word fits in the sentence.
> 3. Look at the pictures surrounding the text to give clues to meanings.

Paired Reading is a time when Manuel has two children read to each other while he analyzes their learning process. To begin, he demonstrates a skill for them and watches how they adapt it. He shows the children how to help each other, first as a listener and then as a person who gives feedback. He suggests that they ask questions and then reread sections that do not make sense. Then the children begin to practice reading aloud to each other.

Manuel has put a great deal of thought and planning into this activity. As he recounts:

> I pair an able-bodied reader with a less fluent reader. I let them change partners once a week. They never stay together any longer than two weeks. I keep the books in this sorter and I have the pairs take them from this sorted space. The names of children are writ-

ten in pairs on a chart nearby and a recording space is provided where they can sign-in for the books they are reading. They are asked to read to each other, to ask questions about the characters, and then to ask about the story.

Although he pairs a strong reader with a weaker reader, in May the difference between children is barely visible. When Manuel works with a pair of readers, he asks children to ask themselves what helps them get meaning from their reading. He reminds them to use illustrations as clues to meaning. He frequently assesses how engaged his students are during Paired Reading, watching their nonverbal behavior, their movements, body position, and gestures.

Manuel has organized the Paired Reading activity so that there is a built-in assessment component for the teacher and students. While he assesses students in his class by observing and recording what he sees as related literacy learning, students are keeping records by writing about what they read.

> While they are reading in pairs, I go around and eavesdrop. I get a general idea of how they really learn and how they read. I know the level of the books they have selected and I can see how fluent they are at a particular level.
>
> Next I check their comprehension in several ways. I do this initially through writing. I have a record sheet that asks them to write something after each book that they read. I ask them to write three sentences telling the main ideas of the story. They should write something about the beginning, the middle, and the end of the story.
>
> Sometimes I ask them to chart the book's story in an open-ended way. On this chart I have spaces for writing in—what is the problem? . . . what is the solution? . . . what is the outcome? I am looking for book talk from each child and I record my understanding of what they do.

Manuel also holds conferences with students about their writing portfolios. The focus of their conversation concerns articulating their thoughts in writing. As they look back over pieces of writing once a month, they can see improvements in their work as new skills in spelling, grammar, and punctuation appear.

Creating a Mental File

Manuel works diligently to create a mental file, as he calls it, on each child. He continually gathers information from a variety of sources to help him assess the language and literacy skills of particular bilingual students in his class. Sometimes he thinks about a particular child as he drives home at night. He subscribes to what Engel calls "keeping track" as a means of documenting a child's growth.

> I think that I am a person who knows what happens on a day-to-day basis. I can keep track in my head and a lot of teachers are really wondering how I keep track and do it. I guess that is really part of my nature. I always want to be kind of connected with every child. I am a person who probably can do it without even jotting down what I see. From the child I develop a feeling that I get as I go along, which I also add to my recording system.

For Manuel, creating a mental file on a bilingual student means observing language and literacy skills and work samples.

Shared Reading/Writing

Shared Reading is the time each day that Manuel instructs the whole class in a large group. He has a daily collection of literacy activities that involve reading and singing, chants, rhymes, big books, and stories on charts he makes. Integrated into the reading activities are different texts and oral exercises, which include practice in decoding words, spelling words, and understanding the grammar in sentences.

Manuel creates tasks that allow children to demonstrate complex thinking skills in literacy areas related to reading and writing. One task involved his reading of the folktale "Mr. Vinegar." The group read the story aloud together, using overhead projection, and then reread it to themselves. Next, they were all asked to use a drawing or a story map to recall the events of the folktale in order. Manuel demonstrated how to draw a story map using the fairy tale "Little Red Riding Hood" to give students a model to work from. He used chart paper and asked children to tell the events of this familiar tale, while he drew representations of them in pictures. The pictures Manuel drew of the characters and places they traveled were put on a winding road, and then words, as labels, were added afterward. The "Mr. Vinegar" activity became an assessment embedded in instruction with a series of steps:

1. Read the story as a group.
2. Read the story in your head.
3. Retell the story events as a group.
4. Create a story map using pictures with words as labels.
5. Write a retelling of the story in your own words and explain the map you created.

Samples of the students' "Mr. Vinegar" writings were displayed in the room, and many were kept for the students' portfolios.

Samples like the Mr. Vinegar story document the many components of language and literacy—retelling a story, translating story meaning into sequential pictures of the events, and then into the student's own words. Using a combination of observation and reflection during Shared Reading and writing activities like this one, Manuel gets a mental picture of each bilingual child's literacy skills from the "snapshots" of literacy events that he has gathered for his mental files. Shared Reading, as Manuel says, "links it all together."

CONCLUSIONS

Manuel, as a bicultural individual, is clearly a literacy model for his bilingual children, since he is always reading and writing for them and with them. Assessment for Manuel means regularly giving his students feedback about what they are doing, how they are doing, and how they can do better. Celebrating the high quality of student work is part of each day, and is one way Manuel links assessment with instruction. He frequently reads aloud samples of work he considers "interesting" or "creative" while a child is in the midst of composing it. He does this so that students can hear the written language of their classmates and build on each other's thinking.

Manuel calls this "sharing the good ideas," and he tries to give each child a time each week to show off an accomplishment. As he puts it, "I try to catch them being good at something." He never shares a child's work without that child's permission, since he is aware of the potential for being singled out and embarrassed. When he publicly recognizes a student's "good work," he explains what he observes in that work, saying, for example, "Here is someone who put their mind to it and shared a powerful idea."

Manuel articulates his view that assessment drives instruction. His words remind us that his goal as a teacher and assessor is to say less and watch more. "When you give them little nudges . . . or a little helping hand, it's as natural as anything. . . . They begin to drive their own learning process."

Assessment Strategies	Classroom Activities
Kid watching learning about children by watching	• observing daily interactions • recording observations using journal • anecdotal notes on activity grid • Paired Reading and Minder
Keeping track collecting data on individual	• questioning students about their work • examining journals • student writing • doing Paired Reading record sheets • interviewing students and parents • conferencing with students around portfolios
Documenting observing and collecting evidence of children's learning	• student portfolios of sample work • Miscue Analysis of Reading—Sept./May • samples of journal pages, reading sheets • student writing folders

7

Conclusions and Implications

My intent with this study was to learn about teachers' judgments in assessing their students following Mitchell's (1992) contention that "teachers need ways of establishing their authority as evaluators of their own students in their own classrooms and having that judgment count for more than a classroom grade" (137).

Studying teachers' classroom interactions has taught me that their judgments *do* count when it comes to understanding the complexities of young bilingual children.

CONCLUSIONS

In each of these six classrooms, bilingual children are assessed using multiple formats and multiple people's perspectives. Preparing to assess bilingual students means extra work for their teachers, including studying issues of language and culture, and planning a classroom to support language learning. In the case studies, Kathy and Manuel describe how they organize their time to integrate this process into their classroom environments.

Teacher Assessment Focus	Considerations	Strategies
social interaction	pairs and large group	observations during day, Paired Reading, Shared Reading
cultural issues	parents, language models, family, social class, culture	observations and samples, journal writing, Writers' Workshop, parent conferences
language and literacy	fluency, comprehension, decoding, work attack skills	observations, Reading Buddies, taped oral reading, Shared Reading, journal and other writings

Figure 7–1

Overall, Kathy, Manuel, and the other teachers use various informal assessments to look closely at what an individual bilingual child knows and can do. They follow a sociocultural pattern of looking first at social interactions, then at issues of culture and language, and finally at specific language and literacy skills, as in Figure 7-1.

All six teachers in this study use "kid watching," "keeping track," and "documentation" to assess bilingual students as part of their daily classroom programs. They combine the assessment strategies charted in Figure 7-2 to collect data on each student's growth in language and literacy skills.

Assessment Strategies	Classroom Activities
Kid watching learning about children by watching	• observing daily interactions • recording using checklists • noting in reading/writing workshop
Keeping track collecting descriptive data on individual	• questioning students about their work • collecting journal pages, reading records • taping oral reading samples • interviewing students and parents • conferencing with students and parents around portfolios
Documenting observing and collecting evidence of children's learning	• writing teacher narrative summaries • keeping portfolios of sample work • taping oral reading quarterly • compiling a binder with samples of journal pages, reading records, monthly self-portraits

Figure 7–2

CLASSROOM ASSESSMENT PRACTICES OF MONOLINGUAL AND BILINGUAL TEACHERS

Of the six teachers in my study, three are monolingual and three are bilingual. A natural question arises: Are there differences in the practice of monolingual and bilingual teachers? This was not one of my research questions, but I did note how these teachers' language background in their respective classrooms played out with regard to assessment practices. The classroom assessment practices of monolingual and bilingual teachers in this study clearly show many more commonalities than differences.

The main differences are related to the use of one or two languages in the classroom. Bilingual teachers indicate that they readily switch to their second language to help explain ideas that they think need further clarification for bilingual students in their classes. Some monolingual teachers also use other children as translators to explain ideas to bilingual students in their native language.

Subtle variations in the emphasis placed on specific practices of monolingual and bilingual teachers were most evident from classroom observations and informal interviews; however, since there are only six teachers involved, these interpretations should be considered tentative and be examined in future research efforts.

Small differences show up in the way monolingual and bilingual teachers initially approach new non-English speakers. Bilingual teachers strive to personally connect to create a relationship with the child; monolingual teachers ask another child to create the beginning relationship by introducing the new child to the classroom environment. Using this buddy system, the new child learns about the physical aspects of the room and its functions, its rules and expectations. These monolingual teachers want new children to fit into their structures, rather than to change the structure to accommodate the new child. Again, this is a hypothesis that needs more data.

Overall, it appears that bilingual teachers are slightly more focused on getting their bilingual students to "understand word meanings" than "to gradually" acquire language and literacy skills. Monolingual teachers appear to be more patient with the language learning process of their non-English-speaking students. Their informal interviews focus on "describing" the extra efforts they make to create a classroom environment to help bilingual students "understand" what to do without English. Carol, Betty, and Kathy (monolinguals) indicate that they interview the parents of new bilingual students daily. They also talk to other staff and community representatives to learn about child rearing and food habits.

Marina, Manuel, and Hannah (bilinguals) indicate that they initially keep bilingual students physically close to them so that they can keep track of what they do and what they understand. They focus on naming survival words for these students right away. This suggests their classroom assessment practices initially place emphasis on the thinking and planning process for bilingual students in their classes. Monolingual teachers appear to focus on working with the social aspects of classroom life, assuming that the academics come later. Bilingual teachers note the importance of social interactions in the classroom, but focus on "communicating" and "vocabulary learning" at the same time.

My classroom observations also revealed differences in second-language use between monolingual and bilingual teachers and their students. In classrooms with bilingual teachers, observations show that during the course of activities, children more often speak two languages. In classrooms where teachers are monolingual, most children speak English with each other during daily classroom activities. During recess, snack time, and free-choice times, bilingual children do, however, speak their native language. This raises the question of whether it is the teacher's permission or modeling that signals how second languages get used in classrooms. Is it that monolingual teachers use one language only, so students follow, whereas bilingual teachers use two languages, so their students do too? This tentative observation warrants further investigation in other settings with more teachers.

EDUCATIONAL IMPLICATIONS

This study has significant educational implications for teacher training of preservice and inservice teachers. Simply stated, primary teachers can be trained to assess bilingual students for instructional purposes. What might this training include? First, teachers can learn a sociocultural approach to classroom assessments that considers the intricate political, social, cultural, and linguistic factors affecting a bilingual learner. Teachers need to consider who this child is as a learner, and how this child learns in a given environment. A child-study process that provides background on the language and the culture of the child should be included in preservice and inservice teacher training. Also, the complex sociocultural factors that affect assessment in classrooms with diverse populations should be made clear to teachers and should be integrated into their daily practice.

Ideally, teachers will learn to withhold quick judgments and will, instead, "sit beside" these learners to observe and document over time what they can do. As a problem solver, the first question a teacher should ask is "Who is this child as a learner?" The next question that the teacher should ask is "What can this student do in a learning environment that facilitates learning without language?"

In a larger sense, this study maps a process and provides a set of tools for teachers' classroom assessment. Culled from the experience of a group of skilled, successful practitioners, the strategies and tools described—observing, interviewing, and collecting and interpreting student work—should be incorporated into teacher training courses.

RESEARCH IMPLICATIONS

The title of this book, *Whose Judgment Counts?*, recognizes the assessment expertise of teachers as well as clinicians. My research documents the voices of teachers engaged in experimenting with classroom assessment and offers the research community an entry into this unexplored field. This study further presents the research community with vital information from teachers who have spent years on their practice and who have succeeded in informally assessing the diverse learners they serve. The case studies of their assessment strategies map the process of linking classroom assessment with instruction. This work is a first step in understanding how teachers informally assess bilingual children in regular classrooms (1) to track progress in language and literacy, and (2) to distinguish language problems from learning problems in bilingual children.

The key to improving assessment practice for bilingual students lies in realigning the power relations in the interpersonal interactions of school communities and recognizing the vital role of teachers as skilled assessors of the children they teach.

In 1922, Chapman had a vision of assessment that explained a sorting process for children in schools (see Figure 1–1, page 3). Chapman's view of assessment for the individual learner omitted vital considerations related to the assessor, the learner, and the process. First, the assessors, the classroom teachers, need to use their own "magnifying glass" to study how individual children learn in a naturalistic context—that is, in a classroom. Second, these teachers need to "widen the lens" of their magnifying glass to uncover the strengths as well as the deficits of a bilingual child. This means that formal assessment tools, which are not designed to deal with classrooms and are not designed to deal with linguistic and cultural differences of bilingual students, are not valid or reliable instruments for this work.

Third, informal assessment that addresses the language and cultural issues of the child requires significant effort from each teacher. It requires preparing for assessing and teaching diverse student populations by first learning who a student is and learning how that student performs in a classroom environment designed for "dealing with differences" *before* considering what that student can achieve. This is a critical point in adapting a sociocultural approach to classroom assessment because it recognizes the complexity in assessing second-language proficiency and cognitive learning in young bilingual children.

Finally, the process of assessing and teaching bilingual students is *ongoing* and requires choosing an appropriate strategy for observing, recording, and collecting the learner's "foot prints" (Wolf 1989). Classroom assessment, as we have learned from this study, is not simple or straightforward. It cannot be specifically defined, nor regulated. It is as complex and intricate as are the individuals it seeks to understand. It is a work in progress. This study may serve as a guide to practitioners who struggle to distinguish language acquisition issues from learning disabilities. Such confusion creates a place where a teacher's judgment can be the judgment that counts. Therefore, it is of paramount importance that teachers be trained to assess bilingual children accurately and that their assessments be seriously considered. They are the hope for the future for bilingual learners.

Methodology

DESIGNING A STUDY OF TEACHERS' CLASSROOM ASSESSMENT

This study was designed to be small and flexible enough to tap into teachers' thinking about assessment and their practice. From my research, I learned that a descriptive study of teachers' classroom assessment could address an existing gap in childhood educational literature, and was a promising pursuit. Therefore, I constructed a qualitative study using interviews and classroom observations to describe the complexity of interactions that take place between teachers and bilingual students in the daily life of classrooms.

As a first step, I defined the context of my study by identifying the factors that affect teachers' assessment practices. Eventually, I decided to study six experienced teachers in the Cambridge Public Schools who were identified by their administrators, principals, and colleagues as being skilled in the assessment of bilingual children.

My next step was to investigate methods that others in the field use to study teachers' classroom assessment practice with bilingual children. I found two related case studies that document elementary teachers' "effective" classroom instruction of bilingual children. Garcia (1991), in a study of three teachers, outlines knowledge, skills, and dispositions that characterize effective instruction for bilingual children. Alvarez, Garcia, and Espinosa (1991) also conducted case studies of two elementary teachers (grades 3 and 5) to identify themes that characterize effective instructional practice for bilingual students.

These studies suggest that effective practice is characterized by teachers who:

1. understand the role of language and culture in the classroom;
2. have clarity around pedagogical views and practices;
3. engage in instructional innovations.

These two case studies provide background for my study of effective teachers' assessment practice and its links to instruction.

The third step was to learn more about the schools and the individual teachers selected. To undersand what problems were faced by teachers in the Cambridge Public Schools, I considered the following factors: (1) primary teachers in the Cambridge Public Schools in the 1990s are in a system that is reforming its primary assessment practice; (2) a primary teacher in an elementary school deals with unique programs and school cultures; and (3) experienced teachers work with as many as four or five language groups in one class.

THE STUDY SETTING: A SCHOOL SYSTEM CHANGING ITS ASSESSMENT PRACTICES

For five years, the Cambridge Public Schools' (CPS) administration and faculty have been, to varying degrees, actively reforming classroom assessment practices at the primary level. Many of the key administrators have contributed to this vision of change. A paper prepared by Lynn Stuart and Jim St. Clair, describing "Documentation and Assessment of Student Progress," provides a summary of ongoing work in K-3 classes in the Cambridge Public Schools (see Appendix).

The goals of this school system's reform efforts echo the nation's goals to strengthen students' abilities to monitor their own progress, teachers' abilities to make informed decisions about their students' levels of understanding, and policy makers' abilities to access accurate accountability data that measures the skills and applications of learning valued by society. The system's proposed Five-Year Plan includes a new documentation plan for assessing student progress, and what staff development will accompany it (see Appendix).

Help in implementing this process of changing views and practices was sought from outside the system. The Lesley College Graduate School of Education became a resource for Cambridge Schools' administrators and teachers. For the last decade, Lesley College has maintained a partnership with CPS, focusing on staff development and teacher training. This partnership impacts classroom practice and professional development by providing:

1. consultants to the CPS Early Literacy Project, with faculty providing on-site staff development in several schools;
2. inservice training of CPS teachers through coursework offered at Lesley at reduced tuition;
3. credit for in-house CPS training of teachers through courses in "Naturalistic Observation" and in "Observation and Recording Children's Behavior";
4. ongoing sponsorship of the Literacy Institute, a weeklong summer workshop for school personnel.

Two individuals were instrumental in formulating the partnership between CPS and Lesley College. Lynn Stuart, as Director of Primary Education in the Cambridge Public Schools, was the school system's leader in creating a new vision of early childhood literacy learning and assessment. Brenda Engel, Study Director of Lesley College, has been the architect of the CPS early childhood assessment reform efforts. Her vision of teaching, learning, and assessment is summarized in *The Handbook of Documentation and Assessment* (1995).

THE FLETCHER, HARRINGTON, AND LONGFELLOW SCHOOLS

My study involves the Fletcher, Harrington, and Longfellow Schools. Each of these schools provides an appropriate setting for inquiry for four reasons:

1. Each teacher's classroom is ethnically and racially integrated (about 50 percent majority students, 50 percent minority), which means that there is a significant population of bilingual children.
2. Teachers are continuously faced with the need to adapt their informal and classroom assessments to meet the needs of incoming bilingual students.
3. A cadre of teachers, administrators, and students has been working to improve teachers' documentation and assessment practice since 1988, and there is systemwide commitment and plan for reform.
4. Teachers have had inservice training in observation and documentation during the past four years, so they are prepared to implement informal assessments, including observations, narratives, and portfolios.

The study was conducted in two phases—the first in 1991-1992, and the second in 1994. Data was collected on six teachers: two kindergarten, two grade 1, and two grade 2. The group included one male and five females, three monolinguals and three bilinguals. In the second phase, additional data was collected on a bilingual Hispanic male teacher and a monolingual European American female teacher. The studies selected for this review focus on young children from preschool to grade 3, and are limited to those related to educational assessment, omitting the areas of psycho-educational, behavioral, and psychological assessment.

The six teachers I chose to work with were selected according to the following criteria:

1. Their work with Limited English Proficient and bilingual students was considered effective by the Primary Director, early childhood resource specialists, and their principals.
2. They were interested in reflecting on their assessment practices, since they were part of the system's documentation study group.
3. I was familiar with their practice; I had worked with two of these teachers.
4. They appeared enthusiastic in my observations of their classrooms and in my interviews with them.
5. They all had at least eighteen years of classroom experience in Cambridge.

All the participating teachers volunteered for this study and were assured of confidentiality. My effective teacher sample includes practitioners recognized for their expertise in assessment, including four who have won awards from professional associations (Apple Teacher Awards, Lucretia Crocker Fellows). As the following chart indicates, two teachers were selected from each school:

School and Teacher Collaborators

SCHOOL	TEACHER	LANGUAGE	GRADE
Fletcher	Manuel	bilingual	2
Fletcher	Carol	monolingual	K
Longfellow	Hannah	bilingual	1/2
Longfellow	Marina	bilingual	K
Harrington	Kathy	monolingual	1/2
Harrington	Betty	monolingual	K

METHODS OF DATA COLLECTION

For data collection, I used three methods: vignette interviews, classroom observations, and informal interviews. Vignette interviews tapped into teachers' thinking about assessment. To examine and explain teachers' classroom assessment practice, I paired observations with informal interviews. These methods allowed me to study simultaneously the processes and the context of teachers' assessment practice.

Vignette Interviews. In these interviews using a vignette, I told teachers about a hypothetical bilingual child and then asked them a series of questions about how they would assess that child's language and literacy skills (see Appendix). The last question allows teachers to tell an actual story about assessing the language and literacy skills of a linguistic minority child who had been in their class. I audiotaped and took notes during interviews, and transcribed them later.

Information from vignette interviews gave me a picture of what these teachers *say* they do to assess bilingual children. To cross-check preliminary findings and document actual classroom interactions, I observed teachers' informal assessment of limited-English-proficient children during daily literacy instruction.

Classroom Observations. My initial observations of the six teachers took place in three schools over a six-week period, during 1991-1992. These classroom observations lasted a minimum of forty-five minutes a day.

During my initial visit to each class, I began by mapping the classroom to note how teachers organize their physical space for group work. Then I noted how long interactions lasted and how long teachers worked with large or small groups. I transcribed my notes within three days so that my memory of the visit would be fresh, and wrote out details on student-teacher and student-student interactions. I wrote a daily memo describing what I learned from each observation, which became a record of my simultaneous data collection and analysis process.

Informal Interviews Connected to Observations. Each day, I conducted informal interviews with teachers immediately following my observations. I asked them to explain their interactions with children. Through taping and transcribing interviews, I gathered detailed information about the structure and the meaning of the spontaneous informal assessments I observed.

During observations, I noticed some teacher-student interactions that I did not understand and that became the focus of my questions. For example, in a bilingual kindergarten, I saw the children signing their names on a chart. Later I learned that as children were signing their names, the teacher was taking attendance and looking at each child's improving ability to write his or her name. She used this "sign-in" format to observe stages of name-writing skills: initials, then first name, then first and last name. After this discussion, she showed me samples of student work and shared her observational notes on the students.

Data Collection for Case Studies as Portraits

During the spring of 1994, I collected an additional twenty-five hours of observations and informal interviews from two of the original six teachers, Manuel and Kathy. I chose to study second-grade teachers, since CPS administrators told me that grade 2 children are most often referred for special education. I chose one monolingual and one bilingual teacher as representative of my sample teachers. My intent was to document examples of informal language and literacy assessment strategies for children and to observe and analyze effective teachers' classroom assessment practices related to ongoing instruction for an extended period of time. In addition, I observed literacy instruction in two classrooms over a three-week period and conducted the same informal interviews described earlier. My portraits describe the classroom assessment practices of two "effective teachers" (one monolingual and one bilingual) that are in keeping with a sociocultural approach.

IMPLICATIONS OF THIS STUDY

I see this study as exploratory and as potentially providing the groundwork for large-scale surveys of teachers with the purpose of developing a sociocultural framework for classroom assessment. Such a study could adapt the vignette interview as a model for hypothetical classroom assessment. Collecting data from a larger cross-section of teachers would refine the definition of classroom assessment practice.

Appendix A

DOCUMENTATION AND ASSESSMENT PLAN

A Brief Summary of Ongoing Work (K–3) in the Cambridge, MA,
   Public Schools
Prepared for the Conference on Alternative Assessment in K–3
   Mathematics, sponsored by TERC, March 1991
Lynn Stuart and Jim St. Clair

Background

For over a decade, the Cambridge Public Schools have been working to adjust curriculum in the early years (K–3) so that it is consistent with a developmental view of learning. The work of Don
Holdaway, Brian Cambourne, Frank Smith, and many others has
helped us to understand the principles of immersion, demonstra-
tion, engagement, community, approximation, and self-regulation
that are present when learning prospers. Underlying all of these

principles is the human drive to construct meaning within the cultural setting(s) in which we live. Also underlying these principles is the understanding that learning takes place over time (which is defined differently for each learner).

When a school district begins to adopt a developmental view of learning, there is a need for institutional reevaluation and change in a variety of areas:

1. Curriculum;
2. Classroom organization and grouping;
3. Intervention (for students who exhibit difficulty);
4. Assessment and Evaluation;
5. Professional development;
6. Parent involvement.

We are currently working on these areas through specific initiatives, but we see them as undeniably interrelated. Considering the effects that current educational assessment practices have on each of these areas, we believe it is necessary to redefine assessment in light of developmental learning principles. In Cambridge, which is an urban community, we have always tried to bring a multicultural perspective to our work. This is particularly important as we discuss new directions.

Our work in the primary grades in the period of 1979 through the mid-eighties focused on natural, developmental literacy acquisition. However, the more developmental our view of language and literacy acquisitions has become, the more we have made connections between literacy and other subject areas, and the more we have explored the possibilities of integrated, thematic learning. The collaboration between the Cambridge Public Schools and Lesley College through the Cambridge/Lesley Literacy Project that began in 1983 has bridged theory and practice in exciting ways.

The five-year longitudinal evaluation study of student progress in literacy at the Longfellow School provided opportunities for researchers (led by Brenda Engel of Lesley College) and teachers to document student progress in detailed, naturalistic ways, based on actual classroom practice and developmental assessment tasks in writing and reading. During this period courses and workshops on naturalistic inquiry were also held for Cambridge teachers. Observation and documentation through work samples were reestablished as prime sources of data. More and more teachers were finding ways to gather documentation for assessment from the everyday activities in their classrooms. Increasingly children began to be included in the data collection. These explorations at the classroom level paved the way for the next steps.

Development of a Systematic, Systemwide Plan for Longitudinal Documentation and Assessment of Student Progress

Two projects in 1988–90 helped to move the school system forward. One was the development of a "strategic plan" for the entire district. A small group of elementary and secondary teachers and administrators worked on a "key result," which would develop and implement portfolio assessment and longitudinal documentation of student progress, K–12. The second project was a yearlong workshop during which a group of primary teachers began to define the purposes and components of a system of keeping track of student learning.

The teachers in the Keeping Track Workshop examined the implications of developmental learning for evaluation:

1. Evaluation of a developmental process should be longitudinal.
2. Assessment methods should take into account the strategies children bring to the task, especially the demand for meaning and the significance of self-correction. Assessment should involve meaningful tasks, not skills in isolation.
3. The best evidence of learning is direct documentation. In order to gain a true picture of a child's learning, many sources of information are necessary.
4. Assessment should improve learning and provide information for making instructional decisions. Evaluation should be built into the teaching/learning process and thus be primarily the responsibility of the teacher and child.

This group of teachers also defined the immediate purposes of keeping track of children's learning:

1. to provide a full picture of each child's learning over time;
2. to provide ongoing information about each child's learning that informs teaching practice;

3. to communicate effectively with parents, administrators, and colleagues;
4. to involve children as assessors of their own learning.

The 1989–90 Keeping Track working group went on to identify the components of a systematic plan for documentation and assessment of student progress in kindergarten through grade 3. A more indepth, yearlong trial by more teachers in 1990–91 is providing further refinement, adaptation, and suggestions for even broader implementation next year.

The *components of the documentation and assessment plan* currently are as follows:

1. **Work samples and student portfolios**—Work in a range of media from all disciplines and integrated studies.
2. **Teacher-kept records**—Observations, inventories, conference notes, and so on.
3. **Student-kept records**—Independent records of reading, writing, reports, logs, journals, portfolio responses, and so on.
4. **Developmental assessment tasks and instruments**—Administered once or twice a year in reading and math.
5. **Documentation Summary**—Student Profile Summary adapted from The Primary Language Record to encompass all aspects of learning (to be completed two times a year, by January and by June).

Appendix B

CRITICAL EDUCATIONAL IMPLICATIONS TO CONSIDER WHEN USING FORMAL ASSESSMENTS

Research shows that:
- bilingual students *take more time* to complete tasks in their second language, so performance on timed tests may be invalid;
- bilingual student may *use a different reasoning strategy* according to their native language, so that a systematic, sequential testing formats may be unfamiliar and of questionable validity;
- careful evaluation of native language proficiency (using both formal and informal assessments) *must precede* any assessment of learning potential;
- decision-making should be made from a collection of formal and informal assessments in the native language (L1) *and* English (L2).

Understand Issues of Language and Culture *"learn about who they are"*	**Create and Environment for Language Learning** *"provide a setting for cross-cultural learning"*
show you accept and value a bilingual learner	organize the physical environment for interactions
research student's cultural and linguistic background	use symbols to translate classroom expectations
acknowledge cultural issues in child-rearing	provide routines in schedules
recognize the cultural transition process and offer support	build assessments into the curriculum

Probe Individual with Informal Assessment Strategies *"discover student's strengths"*	**Monitoring the Individual While Assessing and Teaching** *"note their struggles and breakthroughs"*
observe social interactions	observe student's language and literacy over time
question students while learning	analyze student's learning process
interview students	reflect on student's work using observations and portfolios
develop a portfolio of student work	create a mental file on each child

SUMMARY OF RESEARCH ON INFORMAL ASSESSMENT OF BILINGUAL CHILDREN

Formats for Assessing Language and Cognitive Skills

OBSERVE
- native language use
- second language use
- play interactions
- parent interactions
- teacher interactions

INTERVIEW
- parents
- caretakers
- family members
- peers
- teachers
- school staff

Glossary

BICS refers to basic interpersonal conversational skills defined as those oral language skills that are adequate for classroom social interaction.

Bilingual refers to someone who speaks two languages. In practice bilinguals often have different strengths in their first or native language (L1) than in their second language (L2). Few individuals are balanced bilinguals with equal skills in both L1 and L2. The terms *linguistic minority* and *bilingual* are used interchangeably in the research, but this review reflects the author's terms.

CALPS refers to the complex academic language performance skills, academic language for content learning, including reading and writing.

Cloze Testing refers to an informal assessment used for assessing reading comprehension where single words are omitted from a passage and the reader fills in words that fit the context.

English as a Second Language (ESL) students are in the process of learning English in an instructional setting designed for teaching a second language.

Language or Learning Disabled (LD) children are those who have an identified handicapping condition according to Special Education definitions (Willig and Greenberg 1996).

Limited English Proficient (LEP) refers to nonnative English speakers who are at the early stages of acquiring the language, and have limited oral English language abilities. They are often fluent in their native language.

Linguistic Minority (LM) refers to nonnative English speakers who may be bilingual or limited English proficient children; there is no handicap present, merely a need for language learning.

Performance Tasks are activities that probe what children do and say in a given learning context.

Pragmatic Criteria are defined as observable behaviors in children, and **Structural Criteria** refer to the linguistic components of oral speech.

Pre-Referral Activities are specific classroom assessments used by teachers to better understand the factors that may be contributing to a child's difficulty prior to referring that child for special education assessment and placement.

References

Afflerbach, P., et al. 1995. "Teacher's Choices in Classroom Assessment." *The Reading Teacher* 48: 622-23.

Airasian, P. 1991. *Classroom Assessment.* New York: McGraw-Hill.

Alvarez, L., E. Garcia, and P. Espinoza. 1991. "Effective Instruction for Linguistic Minority Students: An Early Childhood Case Study." *Early Childhood Research Quarterly* 6: 347-61.

Alvarez, M. D. 1988. "Psychoeducational Assessment of Bilingual Students: Current Trends and Major Issues." In *Bilingual Education and English as a Second Language: A Research Handbook, 1986-87,* edited by A. N. Ambert, 221-31. New York: Garland.

————. 1991. "Psychoeducational Assessment of Linguistic Minority Children: Current Perspectives and Future Trends." In *Bilingual Education and English as a Second Language: A Research Handbook, 1988-90,* edited by A. N. Ambert, 233-48. New York: Garland.

Ambert, A. N., ed. 1991. *Bilingual Education and English as a Second Language: A Research Handbook, 1988-90.* New York: Garland.

Anthony, J., T. Johnson, N. Mickelson, and A. Preece. 1991. *Evaluating Literacy*. Portsmouth, NH: Heinemann.

Ariza, M. 1988. Evaluating Limited English Proficient Students' Achievement: Does Curriculum Content in Home Language Make a Difference? Paper presented at the annual meeting of the American Educational Research Association, New Orleans, April.

Au, K. H., J. A. Scheu, A. J. Kawakami, and P. A. Herman. 1990. "Assessment and Accountability in Whole Literacy Curriculum." *The Reading Teacher* 43: 574-78.

Baca, L. M., and E. Almanza. 1991. *Language Minority Students with Disabilities*. Reston, VA: Council for Exceptional Children.

Baca, L. M., and H. T. Cervantes. 1989. *The Bilingual Special Education Interface*. 2d ed. Columbus, OH: Merrill.

Baca, L. M., and C. Clark. 1992. EXITO: A Dynamic Team Assessment Approach for Culturally Diverse Students. Paper presented at the Council of Exceptional Children Conference, Minneapolis, MN, 14 November.

Baca, L. M., and J. S. Valenzuela. 1994. *Reconstructing the Bilingual Special Education Interface*. Washington, DC: National Clearinghouse for Bilingual Education.

Baron, J. B. 1991. SEA Usage of Alternative Assessment: The Connecticut Experience. Proceedings of the Second National Research Symposium on Limited English Proficient Students Issues: Focus on Evaluation and Measurement. Washington, DC: U. S. State Department.

Becker, H. 1990. "Generalizing from Case Studies." In *Qualitative Inquiry in Education: The Continuing Debate,* edited by E. Eisner and A. Peshkin, 231-41. New York: Teachers College Press.

Berman, P. 1995. School Reform and Student Diversity. Case Studies of Exemplary Practices for LEP Students. Santa Cruz, CA: National Center for Research on Cultural Diversity and Second Language Learning.

Bilken, D. 1988. "The Myth of Clinical Judgment." *Journal of Social Sciences* 44 (1): 127-40.

Bracken, B., and N. Fouyad. 1987. "Spanish Translation and Validation of the Bracken Basic Concept Scale." *School Psychology Review* 16 (1): 94-102.

Bredekamp, S., and T. Rosegrant, eds. 1992. *Reaching Potentials: Appropriate Curriculum and Assessment for Young Children.* Vol. 1. Washington, DC: National Association for the Education of Young Children.

Bredo, E., and W. Feinberg. 1982. *Knowledge and Values in Social and Educational Research.* Philadelphia: Temple University Press.

Burkart, G., and K. Sheppard. 1995. *Content ESL Across the USA: Vol. III. A Training Packet.* Washington, DC: Center for Applied Linguistics.

Carrasquillo, A., and V. Rodriguez. 1996. *Language Minority Students in the Mainstream Classroom.* Bristol, PA: Multilingual Matters.

Carrow, E. 1985. *Test for Auditory Comprehension of Language (TALC-R English and Spanish).* Allen, TX: DLM Teaching Resources.

Cazden, C. 1990. In *Achievement Testing in the Early Grades: The Games Grown-ups Play,* edited by C. Kamii, 67. Washington, DC: National Association for the Education of Young Children.

Chang, A. 1988. A Study of Cognitive Development of Preschool Children and Its Implications for Intervention in Singapore. Paper presented at the Australian Development conference, Adelaide, South Australia.

Chang, Y., and D. Watson. 1988. "Adaptations of Prediction Strategies and Materials in a Chinese-English Bilingual Classroom." *The Reading Teacher* 42 (1): 36-44.

Chapman, P. 1988. *Schools as Sorters: Lewis M. Terman, Applied Psychology, and the Intelligence Testing Movement, 1890-1930.* New York: New York University.

Cline, T., and N. Frederickson, eds. 1996. *Curriculum Related Assessment, Cummins and Bilingual Children.* Bristol, PA: Multilingual Matters.

Cloud, N. 1991. "The Acculturation of Ethnolinguistic Minorities." In *Bilingual Education and English as a Second Language: A Research Handbook,* edited by A. Ambert. New York: Garland.

Coballes-Vega, C., and S. J. Salend. 1988. "Guidelines for Assessing Migrant Handicapped Students. *Diagnostique* 13: 64-75.

Cummins, J. 1984. *Bilingualism and Special Education: Issues in Assessment and Pedagogy.* San Diego, CA: College Hill.

———. 1986. "Empowering Minority Students: A Framework for Intervention." *Harvard Educational Review* 56: 18-36.

————. 1989. "A Theoretical Framework for Bilingual Special Education." *Exceptional Children* 65: 111-19.

————. 1991. "Empowering Culturally and Linguistically Diverse Students with Learning Disabilities." ERIC, Digest E500.

Damico, J. S. 1991. "Descriptive Assessment of Communicative Ability in Limited English Proficient Children." In *Limiting Bias in the Assessment of Bilingual Students,* edited by E. V. Hamayan and J. S. Damico. Austin, TX: Pro-Ed.

Damico, J. S., L. Cheng, J. Deleon, J. Ferrer, and F. Westernoff. 1992. Descriptive Assessment in the Schools: Meeting New Challenges with New Solutions. Paper presented at the Council for Exceptional Children, DAS-1992 Conference, Minneapolis, MN, 14 November.

Defina, A. 1992. *Portfolio Assessment: Getting Started.* New York: Scholastic.

Deleon, J. 1990. "A Model for an Advocacy-Oriented Assessment Process in the Psychoeducational Evaluation of Culturally and Linguistically Different Students." *Journal of Educational Issues of Language Minority Students* 7 (Special Issue): 53-67.

Dodson, C. J., and S. J. Thomas. 1988. "The Effect of Total L2 Immersion Education on Concept Development." *Journal of Multilingual and Multicultural Development* 9: 467-85.

Dolson, D. P. 1994. Assessing Students in Bilingual Contexts: Provisional Guidelines. California State Department of Education.

Duran, E. 1991. *Functional Language Instruction for Linguistically Different Students with Moderate to Severe Disabilities.* Reston, VA: ERIC Clearinghouse on the Handicapped and Gifted Children.

Duran, R., and M. Szyanski. 1994. *Improving Language Arts Assessment of Language Minority Students in Cooperative Learning Settings.* Los Angeles, CA: National Center for Research on Evaluation, Standards and Student Testing.

Engel, B., L. Hall, and L. Stuart. 1995. The Handbook of Documentation and Assessment (Cambridge Public Schools). North Dakota: North Dakota Study Group.

Figueroa, R. 1989. "Psychological Testing of Linguistic Minority Students: Knowledge Gaps and Regulations." *Exceptional Children* 56: 145-52.

————. 1990a. "Assessment of Linguistic Minority Group Children." In *Handbook of Psychological and Educational Assessment of Children: Intelligence and Achievement,* edited by D. R. Reynolds and R. W. Kamphaus. New York: Guilford.

————. 1990b. "Best Practices in the Assessment of Bilingual Children." In *Best Practices in School Psychology II,* edited by A. Thomas and J. Grimes. Washington, DC: National Association of School Psychologists.

Fradd, S. H., A. Barona, and M. Santos de Barona. 1989. "Implementing Change and Monitoring Progress." In *Meeting the Needs of Culturally and Linguistically Different Students: A Handbook for Educators,* edited by S. H. Fradd and M. J. Weismantel. San Diego, CA: College Hill.

Fradd, S. H., and J. M. Weismantel, eds. 1989. *Meeting the Needs of Culturally and Linguistically Different Students: A Handbook for Educators.* Boston: Little Brown.

Franklin, E. A. 1988. "Reading and Writing Stories: Children Creating Meaning." *The Reading Teacher* 42: 184-90.

Freeman, Y. 1988. "Do Spanish Methods and Materials Reflect Current Understanding of the Reading Process?" *Reading Teacher* 41: 654-62.

French, R. L. 1991. Portfolio Assessment and LEP Students. Proceedings of the Second National Research Symposium on Limited English Proficient Students Issues: Focus on Evaluation and Measurement. Washington, DC: U. S. State Department.

Gallerano, B. H. 1987. "The Effect of Bilingualism on Child Development: An Investigation in South Tyrol." *Rassegna Italiana di Linguistica Applicata* 18 (3): 29-62.

Garcia, E. 1988. "Bilingual Education in Early Childhood Programs." *Teacher Education and Practice* 41 (1): 31-46.

————. 1991. "Effective Instruction for Language Minority Students: The Teacher." *Boston University Journal of Education* 173 (2): 130-41.

————. 1991. Education of Linguistically and Culturally Diverse Students: Effective Instructional Practice Report. Washington, DC: Center for Applied Linguistics.

————, ed. 1995. *Meeting the Challenge of Linguistic and Cultural Diversity in Early Childhood Education.* Yearbook in Early Childhood series. Vol. 6. Williston, VT: Teachers College Press.

Genesee, F., ed. 1994. *Education and Second Language Children: The Whole Child, the Whole Curriculum, the Whole Community.* New York: Cambridge University Press.

Genesee, F., and E. V. Hamayan. 1994. "Classroom-Based Assessment." In *Education and Second Language Children: The Whole Child, the Whole Curriculum, the Whole Community,* edited by F. Genesee. New York: Cambridge University Press.

Genishi, G., ed. 1992. *Ways of Assessing Children and Curriculum.* New York: Teachers College Press.

Giroux, H. 1988. *Teachers as Intellectuals: Toward a Critical Pedagogy of Learning.* New York: Bergin & Garvey.

Goetz, J., and M. LeCompte. 1984. "Ethnographic Data Collection in Evaluation Research." In *Ethnography in Educational Evaluation,* edited by D. Fetterman. Beverly Hills, CA: Sage.

Goldman, S., and R. Rueda. 1988. "Developing Writing Skills in Bilingual Exceptional Children." *Exceptional Children* 54: 543-51.

Gonzalez, V. 1994. "A Qualitative Assessment Method for Accurately Diagnosing Bilingual Gifted Children." In *NABE Annual Conference Journal,* edited by M. Malave.

Graves, D. H., and B. H. Sunstein. 1992. *Portfolio Portraits.* Portsmouth, NH: Heinemann.

Hakuta, K., and E. Garcia. 1989. "Bilingualism and Education." *American Psychologist* 44: 374-79.

Hamayan, E., and M. Pfleger. 1987. *Developing Literacy in English as a Second Language: Guidelines for Teachers of Young Children from Nonliterate Backgrounds* (Teacher Resource Guide). Washington, DC: Center for Applied Linguistics.

Haney, W., and G. Madaus. 1989. "Searching for Alternatives to Standardized Tests: Whys, Whats, and Withers." *Phi Delta Kappan* 70: 683-87.

Haussler, M., and G. Heald-Taylor. 1987. "Literacy Reading Behavioral Inventory." In *Ideas and Insights: Language Arts in*

Elementary School, edited by D. Watson. Urbana, IL: National Council of Teachers of English.

Hernandez, R. 1994. "Reducing Bias in the Assessment of Culturally and Linguistically Diverse Populations." *The Journal of Educational Issues of Language Minority Students* 14: 269-300.

Jarvis, C. 1988. *Shaping the Future: Teaching Our Youngest Students.* New York: New York Board of Education Office of Assessment.

Jax, V. A. 1988. "Understanding School Language Proficiency Through Assessment of Story Construction." In *Schools and the Culturally Diverse Exceptional Student: Promising Practices and Future Directions,* edited by A. Ortiz and B. Ramirez. Reston, VA: Council of Exceptional Children.

Kamii, C., ed. 1990. *Achievement Testing in the Early Grades: The Games Grown-ups Play.* Washington, DC: National Association for the Education of Young Children.

Koopmans, M. 1987. The Difference Between Task Understanding and Reasoning Skills in Children's Syllogistic Performance. Paper presented at the American Educational Research Association, Washington, DC, April.

LaCelle-Peterson, M., and C. Rivera. 1994. "Is It Real for All Kids? A Framework for Equitable Assessment Policies for English Language Learners." *Harvard Educational Review* 64 (1): 555-75.

Langdon, H. W. 1988. "Gloria: A Bilingual Language/Learning Disabled Student." In *Psychoeducational Assessment of Minority Children: A Casebook,* edited by R. L. Jones. Berkeley, CA: Cobb & Henry.

————. 1989. "Language Disorder or Difference: Assessing the Language Skills of Hispanic Students." *Exceptional Children* 56: 160-76.

Lindholm, K. J. 1988. The Edison Elementary School Bilingual Immersion Program: Student Progress After One Year of Implementation (CLEAR Technical Report Series). California University Center for Language Education and Research.

McLaughlin, B. 1995. *Assessing Language Development in Bilingual Preschool Children.* Washington, DC: National Clearinghouse for Bilingual Education.

Mandel-Morrow, L., and J. Smith. 1990. *Assessment for Instruction in Early Literacy.* Englewood Cliffs, NJ: Prentice-Hall.

Marshall, C., and G. Rossman. 1989. *Designing Qualitative Research.* New York: Sage.

Marshall, S. 1992. "Managing the Culture: The Key to Effective Change." *School Organization* 13: 255-68.

Mathews, J. K. 1990. "From Computer Management to Portfolio Assessment." *The Reading Teacher* 43: 421.

Maxwell, J. A., and B. Miller. In press. "Two Aspects of Thought and Two Components of Qualitative Data Analysis." *International Journal of Qualitative Studies.*

Maxwell, J. M. 1992. "Validity in Qualitative Research." *Harvard Educational Review* 62: 279-95.

Mehen, H., A. Hertweck, and J. L. Meihls. 1986. *Handicapping the Handicapped: Decision Making in Students' Educational Careers.* Palo Alto, CA: Stanford University Press.

Meisels, S., and D. Steele. 1991. *The Early Childhood Portfolio Collection Process.* Ann Arbor: University of Michigan Center for Human Growth and Development.

Merriam, S. 1988. *Case Study Research in Education: A Qualitative Approach.* San Francisco: Jossey-Bass.

Miles, M., and A. M. Huberman. 1984. *Qualitative Data Analysis: A Sourcebook of New Methods.* Newbury Park, CA: Sage.

Mishler, E. 1988. *Research Interviewing: Context and Narrative.* Cambridge, MA: Harvard University Press.

Mitchell, R. 1992. *Testing for Learning: How New Approaches to Evaluation Can Improve American Schools.* New York: Free Press.

Nuttall, E. V. 1987. "Survey of Current Practices in the Psychological Assessment of LEP Children." *Journal of School Psychology* 25: 53-61.

O'Malley, J. M., and L. V. Pierce. 1996. *Authentic Assessment for English Language Learners: Practical Approaches for Teachers.* Chicago, IL: Addison-Wesley.

Organization for Economic Cooperation and Development (OECD). 1992. *Multicultural Education.* Paris, France: Center for Educational Research and Innovation (CERI).

Ortiz, A., and S. Garcia. 1989. "A Prereferral Process for Preventing Inappropriate Referral of Hispanic Students to Special Education." In *Schools and the Culturally Diverse Exceptional Students*, edited by A. Ortiz and B. Ramirez. 2d ed. Reston, VA: Council of Exceptional Children.

Ortiz, A., and E. Polyzoi. 1988. "Language Assessment of Hispanic Learning Disabled and Speech and Language Handicapped Students: Research in Progress." In *Schools and the Culturally Diverse Exceptional Students: Promising and Future Dimensions*, edited by A. Ortiz and B. Ramirez. Reston, VA: Council of Exceptional Children.

Padilla, A. M., C. Valadez, and M. Chang. 1988. Young Children's Oral Language Proficiency and Reading Ability in Spanish and English (CLEAR Technical Report). Berkeley, CA: University Center for Language Education and Research.

Parratore, J. 1995. Teaching Literacy to Bilingual Children: Effective Practices for Use by Monolingual and Bilingual Teachers. Paper presented at the Annual Meeting of the National Association for Bilingual Education.

Perrone, V., ed. 1991. *Expanding Student Assessment*. Alexandria, VA: Association for Curriculum and Supervision.

Pierce, L. Valdez, and J. M. O'Malley. 1992. Performance and Portfolio Assessment for Language Minority Students. (Program Information Guide Series, 9.)

Rado, M., and L. Foster. 1987. The Language Environment of Children with a Non-English Speaking Background. Paper presented at the Ethnicity and Multiculturalism National Conference, Melbourne, Australia, April.

Ramirez, B. 1990. "Perspectives on Language Proficiency Assessment." In *Children at Risk: Poverty, Minority Status, and Other Issues in Educational Equity*, edited by A. Barona and E. E. Garcia. Washington, DC: National Association of School Psychology.

Ramirez, B., and A. Ortiz, eds. 1989. *Schools and Culturally Diverse Exceptional Students: Promising Practices and Future Trends*. Reston, VA: Council for Exceptional Children.

Rhodes, N. 1991. *Project-Assessing Academic Language of Language Minority Students*. Washington, DC: Center for Applied Linguistics.

————. 1993. *Literacy Assessment: A Handbook of Instruments.* Portsmouth, NH: Heinemann.

Roden, G. 1988. "Handicapped Immigrant Preschool Children in Sweden." *Western European Education* 20 (3): 95-107.

Rueda, R., and E. Garcia. 1996. "Teachers' Perspectives on Literacy Assessment and Instruction with Language Minority Students: A Comparative Study." *Elementary School Journal* 96: 311-22.

Salend, S. J. 1990. "A Migrant Education Guide for Special Educators." *Teaching Exceptional Children* 22 (2): 18-21.

Saville-Troike, M. 1988. "Private Speech: Evidence for Second Language Learning Strategies During the Silent Period." *Journal of Child Language* 15: 567-90.

————. 1991. Teaching and Testing for Academic Achievement: The Role of Language Development. Focus, Occasional Papers in Bilingual Education, National Association of Bilingual Education.

Schiff-Myers, N. B., et al. 1994. "Assessment Considerations in the Evaluation of Second Language Learners: A Case Study." *Exceptional Children* 60: 237-48.

Scruggs, T., and M. Mastropieri. 1995. "Assessment of Students with Learning Disabilities: Current Issues and Future Directions." *Diagnostique* 20 (4): 17-31.

Shafer, S. M. 1988. "Bilingual Bicultural Education for Maori: Cultural Preservation in New Zealand." *Journal of Multilingual and Multicultural Development* 9: 487-501.

Snow, C. E. 1992. "Perspectives on Second Language Development: Implications for Bilingual Education." *Educational Researcher* 21 (2): 16-20.

Spodek, B., and O. Saracho, eds. 1991. *Issues in Early Childhood Curriculum.* New York: Teachers College Press.

Stefanakis, E. H. 1991. "Early Childhood Education: The Effects of Language on Learning." In *Bilingual Education and English as a Second Language: A Research Handbook, 1988–1990,* edited by N. Ambert, 139-147. New York: Garland.

————. 1993. A Review of the Literature on the Assessment of Young Linguistic Minorities. Unpublished qualifying paper, Harvard Graduate School of Education.

Stiggins, R. 1987. "Design and Development of Performance Assessments." *Educational Measurement: Issues and Practice* 6 (3): 33-42.

Stiggins, R., N. Conklin, and N. Bridgeford. 1986. "Classroom Assessment: A Key to Effective Instruction." *Educational Measurement: Issues and Practice* 5 (2): 5-17.

Tierney, R., M. Carter, and L. Desai. 1991. *Portfolio Assessment in the Reading Writing Classroom.* Norwood, MA: Christopher-Gordon Publishers.

Valencia, S. 1990. "A Portfolio Approach to Classroom Reading Assessment: The 'Whys, Whats, and Hows'." *The Reading Teacher* 43: 338-40.

Valencia, S., E. Heibert, and P. Afflerbach. 1994. "Realizing the Possibilities of Authentic Assessment: Current Trends and Future Possibilities." In *Authentic Reading Assessment,* edited by S. Valencia, E. Heibert, and P. Afflerbach. Newark, DE: International Reading Association.

Verma, M., ed. 1995. *Working with Bilingual Children: Good Practice in the Primary Classroom.* England: Multicultural Matters.

Vilke, M. 1988. "Some Aspects of Early Second-Language Acquisition." *Journal of Multilingual and Multicultural Development* 9 (1-2): 115-28.

Wiggins, G. 1993. *Assessing Student Performance: Exploring the Purposes and Limits of Testing.* San Francisco: Jossey-Bass.

Wilcox, K. A., and S. Aasby. 1988. "The Performance of Monolingual and Bilingual Mexican Children on the TACL." *Language Speech and Hearing Services in Schools* 19: 34-41.

Wilkinson, C. 1992. Curriculum Based Assessment. Paper and workshop presented at the Council for Exceptional Children Conference, Minneapolis, November.

Wilkinson, C., and W. Holzman. 1988. Relationships Among Language Proficiency, Language Test of Administration, and Special Education Eligibility for Bilingual Hispanic Students with Suspected Learning Disabilities. Paper presented at the annual meeting of the American Educational Research Association, New Orleans, April.

Willig, A. C., and H. F. Greenberg. 1986. *Bilingualism and Learning Disabilities.* New York: American Library.

Willig, D. K., and C. M. Sweeting. 1986. "Assessment of Limited English Proficient Hispanic Students." *School Psychology Review* 15: 59-75.

Wolf, D. P. 1989. "Portfolio Assessment: Sampling Student Work." *Educational Leadership* 46 (7): 35-39.

Yin, R. 1984. *Case Study Research: Design and Methods.* New York: Sage.